P9-AFO-283

How Phenomena Appear to Unfold

How Phenomena Appear to Unfold

Leslie Scalapino

Potes & Poets Press Inc. Elmwood, Connecticut. 1989

Acknowledgments:

All of the essays in this book (except for "Note on My Writing") were
originally given as talks: at Intersection, New College of California, New
Langton Arts, Small Press Distribution, and the Naropa Institute. "Pat-
tern—And the 'Simulacral' ", "Re-living," and "Poetic Diaries" were
published in the *Poetics Journal. Fin de siècle, III* was published in
Temblor. The three *fin de siècle* plays are parts of one work in progress.
"Picasso and Anarchism" was published in *Tyuonyi*. The author wishes to
thank Philip Whalen for his participation and for allowing his taped
conversation to be published in the essay "How Phenomena Appear To
Unfold."

This publication has been partially funded by the National Endowment for
the Arts, a federal program.

Cover illustration courtesy of The Rockwell Museum, Corning, New
York.

Copyright © 1990 Leslie Scalapino
ISBN 0–937013–30–7

For my parents,
Dee Jessen Scalapino and Robert Scalapino

Contents:

fin de siècle
a play

FIN DE SIÈCLE
A PLAY

The play is performed by two men. They sit on crates facing out, not towards each other. The poems are spoken by pausing at line breaks and dashes, as if they were songs. They speak simply clearly modestly. Behind them is a painted backdrop of expanse of savanna.

I will be—as a construction
1. —worker
held under—in the world
as a permanent lower class

> that is—as the
> construction—
> worker—not so

that that will be the same—as my own mind—and
it is so—free—with the rest crushing and regarding as
inferior which is nothing there is not that

> there is not that

> their people—riding on the steppes—
> 2. there isn't anything—but
> grass barren vast.

> > we're always asked
> > to take care of
> > 1. this other person who is
> > weak and is
> > superior and regarded as
> > that

11

worker asked to
2. take care of the rest who're strong
and who're seen as that

          the construction worker is
          extended so there is nothing
1.   them—by them—who're
          strong

                       who're
                       weak

goaded so that reaction
is the same—as my
own mind
inside

          sometimes I wish being a construction
          worker
          I were just condemned once and for all
          to a permanent lower class

a scorching day—walking—and men
on a ladder
2. are up—painting a sign
on a storefront—so work
is inside—them

          —them
          inside is movement so
          walking who's person
1.   by goes
          car—by goes cycle
          weather scorching
          the—in—painting men

                       many—very—little
                       words, see

2. free

> that means being
> defined—by them—but
>
> 1. if they're not defined by them
>   which they aren't—they aren't
>   their class—there is not that

everything is simply doing
as hammering riding
driving

> of—the—riding
> set
> and—don't know
> anything
> about riding

graffiti on wall do
something with a clear
2. conscience burn a cop
cars going by

> that—is
> 1. inside—
>   him

> reach up with
> net, and shown
> by other
> not to catch flying
> jeweled insect

we haven't changed any
from the time of Gengis Khan
we have a fin de siècle
weariness

no, struggle again to
turn insect jeweled
which is flying
not *it*

they're in the corporation
2. —that are mute
that are out in the breeze
at night

and if you mutilate
1. people—they'll
be beggars

school says inferior
construction
2. worker—for it's
a corporation, so *not*
go to it

I'm walking and
this man out says to me
look at that outfit sneering

misery in
corporations and then
1. inefficiency having not
dunned patients

I'm
getting old, not just to know
one'll die but to be outside

going by
(sung   boys who're kneeding
gently) and molding the dung
slapped on the walls
gone from it

the hospital foundering on not
dunning the patients
on time

their in
that

very heavy
2. with child—in the person
walking out

to turn skater
gladiators—cycle
of the merger
of—successive poor
groups

knees up—flesh of on the
bicycle
crew—though of the one in the
flash of them going around the corner
in it

they just don't think that
whether the person is mutilated
1. from stealing matters not
whether there's enough—or
is on the street

in
around
the ring kneeing
another—or
going by

                                        legs
                                        back—around
                                        the ring
                                        their
                                        forward

men crouched or
standing in doorway so they're
floated from their view grainy
there

                    —just in them
              2.   love—in
                    their—in the
                    construction

                                   not even
                                   then

the one construction
worker—or man
painting on the storefront—is
just there without the relation to
the others

                                        it had to
                              1.   do
                                        with turning it

they're weak that are out
2.   or the men painting on
      the storefront that
      riding is inside

                    weak
                    is
                    —in them
                    that has
                    nothing

16

they're weak that are in the
breeze walking
at night the warm weather and
ecstatic

      developments
      waves of them on
      hills in them

a ship sailing, pulling
away from dock—its wake
and a man part of the mess crew
in it—working—it on the
mass of water

      put back through
      that's
      not going to seem

small child romping on the hill
like lambs
1. and newborns and
the adults happy at
the ones

      man murdered because he's
      in a section
      not supposed to be in and is
      understandable

      the construction worker says
      the person being murdered
      being in that section is understandable

      he says
      this

on bicycle—crew—only there's the
2.   one in it as their flash around
corner

turn that out
—to—the one being outside
who is in
the bicycle crew, which is inside

        flash—of that
        outside
        serene
        which is of
        the one as their there

                to have to care for
                that which he says is
                strong or weak

Note on My Writing

NOTE ON MY WRITING
On *that they were at the beach—aeolotropic series.*

The ship (so it's in the foreground)—with the man who's the beggar in back of it, the soil is in back of him—is active. So it's mechanical—there aren't other people's actions—I don't know how old the man in back is. Who's older than I, desire'd been had by him for something else. I'm not old.

And with him being inactive back then.

Playing ball—so it's like paradise, not because it's in the past, we're on a field; we are creamed by the girls who get together on the other team. They're nubile, but in age they're thirteen or so—so they're strong.

(No one knows each other, aligning according to race as it happens, the color of the girls, and our being creamed in the foreground—as part of it's being that—the net is behind us).

I intended this work to be the repetition of historically real events the writing of which punches a hole in reality. (As if to void them, but actively).

Also, to know what an event is. An event isn't anything, it isn't a person.

No events occur. Because these are in the past. They don't exist.

Conversely as there is no commentary external to the events, the children on the playing field can commune with each other. It is entirely from the inside out.

There was when writing the work something else occurring besides what's going on in the segments. But the events do not represent that.

A segment in the poem is the actual act or event itself—occurring long after it occurred; or acts put into it which occurred more recently. They somehow come up as the same sound pattern.

The self is unraveled as an example in investigating particular historical events, which are potentially infinite.

21

The self is a guinea pig.

The piece in *that they were at the beach* titled "A Sequence" is erotica, a genre being artificial which can 'comment on itself' as a surface because it is without external commentary.

External commentary does not exist as it's being entirely erotica genre, which is what?

By its nature as erotica genre, it is convention. Though it may not have people's character or appear to be social convention. Nor does there appear to be domination.

In a Godard film such as *Hail Mary*, one doesn't know whether it is just its surface or it is from the inside out.

Similarly, in "A Sequence" the surface(s) is (are) the same.

The camera lens of writing is the split between oneself and reality. Which one sees first—view of dying and life—is inside, looking out into untroubled 'experience.'

Which is the beggar who's lying back from the dock (in the above example).

So that repression would not be a way of giving depth.

"Chameleon series" in *that they were at the beach* are (multiple) cartoons, distortions of the (inner) self, which have a slight quality of refined Medieval songs.

Interpreting phenomena is deciphering one's view. This is related to poems which are cartoons or writing which uses the genre of comic books, as commentary being the surface.

The form has the 'objective' quality of life—i.e. the comic book, from which life is excluded, has freedom in the actions of the 'characters.'

*

A recent work of mine in such a chameleon cartoon mode is a short 'novel' titled *THE PEARL*. It is the form of the comic book as writing. Each line or paragraph is a frame, so that each action occurs in the moment.

The writing does not have actual pictures. It 'functions' as does a comic book—in being read.

And read aloud to someone the picture has to be described or seen and then what the figure in it says read.

So it's private.

Cartoons are a self-revealing surface as the comic strip is continuous, multiple, and within it have simultaneous future and past dimensions.

Being inside each frame, is the present moment. But at the same time the writing (the frame) is really behind, in the rear of 'what is really occurring.' The things are happening out ahead of the writing.

The following is five or more frames:

And there's this pink sky that's in front but as if—beforehand.

To the events (of that night) that entire day goes, and then there's this incredible vast corrugated rungs of rose colored yet extreme sunset as if it had covered the sky and is behind it, pushing.

She's driving up the street of small flat porched houses and it's behind her, and stretching in front as well.

And as if the events are pushed—from it.

What's happened—?—she'd slept during the day. Checking the man's apartment, he's not there.

What is in the frame is occurring—but what's going on (which is 'free') is ahead of, being pushed by, the writing.

The title is a reference to the Medieval poem *The Pearl*. But the work is made up, from experience.

There are similar possibilities in using the form of plays composed of poems. These are 'experience' in that the surface is the same: each poem is an act, done by the actor. It takes place exactly in and as that moment.

The actors, as for example in the play *fin de siècle*, can be made to be something other than what they are. Which causes that thing to be gently internalized by them. People don't usually speak in poems. They aren't that. Nobody's any thing.

The setting and tone of these plays are both realistic and artificial.

Pattern — and the 'Simulacral'

PATTERN—AND THE 'SIMULACRAL'

The way things are seen in a time is that period of time; and is the composition of that time. The way things are seen is unique in any moment, as a new formation of events, objects, and cultural abstraction.

> The composition is the thing seen by every one living in the living they are doing, they are the composing of the composition that at the time they are living is the composition of the time in which they are living. It is that that makes living a thing they are doing. Nothing else is different, of that almost any one can be certain. The time when and the time of and the time in that composition is the natural phenomena of that composition.[1]

Stein's conception of a continuous present is when everything is unique, beginning again and again and again. A does not equal A, in terms of Stein's view of the continuous present. This leads to lists; which leads to romanticism in which everything is the same and therefore different.

> Romanticism is then when everything being alike everything is naturally simply different, and romanticism

Romanticism is not a confusion but an extrication. Culture is a transformative composite separate from individuals. The quality in the creation of expression in the composition has to do with the unique entity, being in balance and moving as it ceases to be identical with itself. This has to do with apprehending what occurs now. With it being *always* now, which constitutes being in a state of turmoil:

> There must be time that is distributed and equilibrated. This is the thing that is at present the most troubling and if there is the time that is at present the most troublesome the time-sense that is at present the most troubling is the thing that makes the present most troubling.

The present is the loci (i.e., multiple) of change. The travel book as a genre is a stylized mode having its own laws and pattern, which is realistic with present-time events and people: Hemingway, in *Green Hills of Africa*, creates a new form while using the travel book format describing

---

[1] This and the following two quotations are from Gertrude Stein, "Composition as Explanation," *Selected Writings of Gertrude Stein* (New York, 1962).

an actual hunting expedition which lasted for a month.[2] It is not fiction; there is no beginning, middle, or end as such. There are potentially an infinite number of animals and events as the condition of writing.

Therefore his pattern is a list of places, objects, animals, and actions. Reading is somehow the means of their actual occurrence.

Style is cultural abstraction—i.e., that period—how relationships with people take place (how they're seen) in a period. They become visible by being simplified—by indicating this is occurring—as the canned scenario.

The narrator does not write while hunting, only reads. Therefore action is "doing something you are ignorant about." Killing is romanticism everything being the same and therefore different, the trigger of the gun being "like the last turn of the key opening a sardine can." A unique connection, in its sense of the artificial and as such realistic, is the vulcanized rubber faintly transparent looking (as if miming) rhino discovered in death. As the relation between life and writing:

> The rhino was in high grass, somewhere in there behind some bushes. As we went forward we heard a deep, moaning sort of groan. Droopy looked around at me and grinned. The noise came again, ending this time like a blood-choked sigh. Droopy was laughing. "Faro," he whispered and put his hand palm open on the side of his head in the gesture that means to go to sleep. Then in a jerky-flighted, sharp-beaked little flock we saw the tick birds rise and fly away. We knew where he was and, as we went slowly forward, parting the high grass, we saw him. He was on his side, dead.

In *Green Hills of Africa*, the pattern of experience and the account (expressed as being the mode of 'genre') are not parallel; which makes this text similar to the dissimulation and simulacra of artists of the postmodern period.

The closure of the genre is its means of realistic observation.

In Michael McClure's work,[3] oneself is the 'simulacra' identified as an infinite free universe. Identity is defined in his poems in terms of other entities (we are "DARK FLESH MUSIC/LAYING OUT A SHAPE," we are "INSTRUMENTS / THAT / PLAY / ourselves," etc.). Therefore the author or the sense of self and the investigation of its desire is the pattern,

---

[2] Ernest Hemingway, *Green Hills of Africa* (New York, 1935).
[3] Michael McClure, *Selected Poems* (New York, 1986); and *Hymns to St. Geryon & Dark Brown* (San Francisco, 1980).

which is neither present time nor the past. It is potentially infinite in form and number, as points of intuitional apprehension.

Use of pattern as cartoons is investigation of fantasy and active creation of cultural abstractions.

Cultural abstractions such as the love image of Jean Harlow or the perfect chill slot of space of Wall Street (in "Cold Saturday Mad Sonnet") are qualitative transformations as expressions of this instant of time in the poem. In the following passage from "La Plus Blanche," the juncture of connection is "How," and the new utterly wild formation is something referred to as "grace."

> you return love. Love returned for admiration! Strangeness
> is returned by you for desire. How. Where
> but in the depth of Jean Harlow is such strangeness
> made into grace?

Some of McClure's poems are 'genre' in the sense of being formal as sonnets, odes, or ballads but actually as unique, as artificial, not the same as anything else. Therefore the new formations can't be replicated, as are images of Pop Art or as would be commercial images. They are sensitive. The imagination causes transformations, realistic as culture causing mutations. The 'transformations' in the "Hummingbird Ode" are the "black lily of space," the "sweetness of the pain," and "the beautiful shabby colors / and the damp spots where the eyes were" of the dead hummingbird:

> WHAT'S
> ON YOUR SIDE OF THE VEIL?
> DID YOU DIP YOUR BEAK
> in the vast black lily
> of space? Does the sweetness
> of the pain go on forever?

Dark Brown, for example, is writing as a self-analyzing surface which is vision. One is lost in the 'simulacra': "The tygers of wrath are wiser than the horses of instruction—/ means that the belief of something is necessary to its beauty." As in a Busby Berkeley follies, change or movement is by virtue of the intrinsic qualities of something: "The flow of energy through a system acts to organize that system."

In Ron Silliman's *Paradise* the unit of change occurs on the level of the sentence, many such changes occurring in each paragraph.[4] A series or list of simple sentences creates simple states of being, requiring that consciousness exist only in the moment of each sentence, i.e., in an infinite series of succeeding moments. That experience actually occurs in the lovely light 'clear' writing. An overt simplification or abstraction of a view of character, either reader's or writer's, is imposed to create these states of being, which may be the expression of a period or an inward state:

> In romance, sexual desire is freed from a relation to power. The real bandit queen or India, Madame Gandhi. Puffball clouds in a blue sky. Simple sentences, again and again. The old sisters walk to the store together, slowly, one wearing bright slippers. Our lives are like this, quiet on a Sunday. Sink full of cups.

Reading as imposing syntax, is creating reality as imposition on or formation of one's thoughts and actions:

> This was and now you are constituted in the process of being words, your thought actualizing through the imposition of this syntax. Resistance alone is real (coming distractions). Cross against the light. Leave work to write a poem and not mention the dragonfly.

New formations as words, fantasies, sounds, occur potentially infinitely. The 'directorial intelligence' is seen to be either author or context or the one as the other. Therefore our being replications or something being replicated takes place 'visibly' as an action.

So the process of cultural abstraction itself is the model or mechanism for the pattern. Reading imposing a reality on us is therefore the "response card referred to as the action." Deciphering oneself entails what one is; the concept of that entails the action of what the text is. We mime the simulacra, "syntax mimes space," in order to get at the real.

A variation on the notion of apprehending the inherent nature of a being, object, or event as motion is suggested by the Busby Berkeley follies or a dance concentrating on one point or juncture repeated but never the same, which cannot remain identical with itself.

In the example of a centralized pattern, the Busby Berkeley follies with skits or vignettes without necessarily a beginning, middle, or end: the pattern is submitted to the control of an overriding authority, but with the

---

[4] Ron Silliman, *Paradise* (Providence, R.I., 1985).

notion that the finely tuned unit would avoid the distortion of the whole. Using the notion of the pattern being the inherent nature of something as movement, the model of such writing while possibly using a 'format' ('genre'), would be tuned to change occurring on every level. As suggested by a model from physics, the individual person, general context of nature, social behavior, and specific event are undergoing change in one moment. The same scene will not be repeated.

> The same pattern of things is not necessarily repeated at all levels; and secondly, we are not even supposing that the general pattern of levels that has been so widely found in nature thus far must necessarily continue without limit.[5]

A variation and extension of aspects of the discussion suggested here may be seen in Cindy Sherman's work.[6] Her early photographs refer to scenes or atmosphere from thirties or forties movies: an example of a projection of aping of a genre or mode fixed in time—but taken seriously in its establishing its own version or reality—therefore that which duplicates can't be easily duplicated.

Her work to date is a series of replicas—the subject is always Cindy Sherman herself, yet they are not self-portraits. The photographs become increasingly unrecognizable as to their subject. One photograph, for example, is a masculine figure wet gravel on its face seemingly having died recently, but on closer observation showing sores indicating the beginnings of decomposition; another figure is a blonde-wigged woman propped on her elbows on pebbles with her mouth open showing a bright red liquid blood-like interior. The use of costumes, overtly staged and stagey scenes produces a potentially infinite series of new characters.

Therefore the question as to the identity of the author and of oneself is apparently the subject—that conception itself being an expression or 'analysis' of postmodernist sensibility, i.e., the photographs overtly expressed as cultural abstraction or the critical conceptualization of the present art scene.

The following passage as an example of this critical conceptualization is from an essay by Rosalind Krauss, titled "A Note on Photography and the Simulacral":

[5] David Bohm, *Causality & Chance in Modern Physics* (Philadelphia, 1971).
[6] Cindy Sherman, *Cindy Sherman* (New York, 1984); exhibit at the Metro Gallery, New York, 1986.

That Sherman is both subject and object of these images is important to their conceptual coherence. For the play of stereotype in her work is a revelation of the artist herself as stereotypical. It functions as a refusal to understand the artist as a source of originality, a fount of subjective response, a condition of critical distance from a world which it confronts but of which it is not a part....If Sherman were photographing a model who was not herself, then her work would be a continuation of this notion of the artist as a consciousness that knows the world by judging it. In that case we would simply say that Sherman was constructing a critical parody of the forms of mass culture. With this total collapse of difference, this radical implosion, one finds oneself entering the world of the simulacrum....If the simulacrum resembles anything, it is the Idea of nonresemblance. Thus a labyrinth is erected, a hall of mirrors, within which no independent perspective can be established from which to make distinctions—because all of reality has now internalized those distinctions.[7]

The criticism as description, using Krauss's essay as an example, is the process of creating convention—the description of ourselves as culture. Sherman's work is the convention and the revelation of that; as such, the focus is the mystery of the convention which is nonresemblance itself, i.e., originality or subjectivity.

The unit as the book—the book as a unit
Examples of Sherman as unrecognizable subject: a photograph of a large figure with a long red artificial sensual tongue in the foreground behind which are ant-size humans; a shot of a head with a pig's snout, blood-like smears on the snout and cheek, the figure lying on a dark background. Another photograph shows a sweat-covered or moist figure unrecognizable as to gender crouching clutching or sorting through pebbles, looking up at the camera with a wild expression showing a mouth of rotten teeth. The costume dramas in the collection, coming at the end of the series cause the sequence of photographs to seem to fly apart.

Charles Bernstein's *The Sophist* presents a multiplicity and potentially endless proliferation of voices and characters.[8] In terms of the use of genre:

The poem "Fear and Trespass" is an example of being entirely inside

[7.] Rosalind Krauss, "A Note on Photography and the Simulacral," *October* 31 (Winter 1984): 49-68.
[8.] Charles Bernstein, *The Sophist* (Los Angeles, 1987)

some other voice. The details of the circumstance of the couple in this piece are never given; but the circumstance is conveyed in a deliberately bathetic language of Harlequin romance or soap opera. Bathos and turgid vocabulary are as valid as any other information. There is no introspective or conscious voice which would have a different or outside perspective; in that sense the form of the writing goes beyond or outside the confines of the convention of a 'poem' and is someone's else's 'book.' The piece is language as a jostling whipped-up surface—its motion is entirely in that, in terms of it being the whipped-up singular perspective. So it is not simply satire.

Other examples of the use of 'genre'—which therefore unlike the model: "The Only Utopia Is in a Now" uses a voice or perspective reminiscent of eighteenth-century genre describing people's attitudes and behavior, and criticizing their manners and morals. The authorial voice criticizes the inhabitants of this imaginary utopia by assimilating their constructs of emotion and anti-emotion:

> You see, emotion doesn't express itself only in words we already know. But people here who talk about emotion don't really want to experience it. They only want simulations of it in patterns of words they've already heard.

Other examples of 'genre' are ostensible imitation of some other writer, as in "From Lines of Swinburne," in which the poem speaks of itself as a voice—maintaining that singular perspective—as aping itself, being a play on itself. The writing is different from either the old model or the present conception of a poem.

Poems may in *The Sophist* actually be plays, as in the piece titled "Entitlement," in which named characters speaking to each other—things being like something else—simply make statements of those resemblances, rather than having dramatic situations or action. The statements of resemblances are an aping of actions.

In "The Last Puritan," a hypothetical character is projected as "anything merely seen or heard." A single poem or prose piece may have multiple voices or perspectives. The voice in a piece may seem to be the author's, or there may be a variety of characters, or simply voices interweaving ideology, information, commentary on the writing, or contradiction of previously declared opinions or assertions. The text uses words that aren't real or are hybrids or deliberately misspelled; its language also consists of blank spaces, slang, nonsense sounds, capitalization of parts of words; the text introduces as one character a Mr. Bernstein who turns out not to be the author: it introduces someone else's book, *The Odyssey*, misquoting it. Word and object are expressions or formal projections of each other.

Bernstein comments in reference to the proliferation of perspectives or detail: "There is never annul / ment, only abridgement." Nothing is left out of the writing; so it goes past the confines of a 'book.' Distortion of the individual unit by the whole is part of the writing's acknowledged mode; comparable to Peter Schjeldahl's notion, in his introduction to Sherman's work, of "Presence" as emerging in the costume dramas with the photographer finally being there as only herself the actress.

The order of *The Sophist* is carefully composed to create "a single but layered structure." The book does not have a beginning, middle, and end as would occur in the unfolding of a drama or story. As in the play "Entitlement," which consists of statements of resemblances, there is no progression of development of a plot. The poem, "the order of a room," is a series of statements or types of order:

a geometric order
a cosmetic order
a temporal order
public order

Some of the ways of seeing the structure or order of the 'book' are "hypostatization of space, the relations detemporalized," "idea of explaining the visible world by a postulated invisible world," distance, arrangement of letters on the page, blanks that could be filled in thereby changing the order, abbreviations, etc. In terms of a geometric model, the notion is of the 'book' being detemporalized and spatial.

Aping doing imitations (as in the Swinburne poem) is an example of incorporating a sense of relativity in terms of time.

The book is the "single but layered structure"—the notion of "a body that seemed genuinely music"—given more as the *idea* of a music than the actual formal rendition and sound of that music. In other words, the latter occurs as the abstract configuration of the idea.

Similar to aspects of Stein's view of composition or Hemingway's cultural abstraction in *Hills*, yet seeing experience differently from them (for example, all times operating at the same time, a different sort of cultural analysis), Bernstein's work projects a symphonic structure that

34

would reflect multiple changes occurring in the present instant. Such a projected work need not be seen as a dissipated version of modernism or as leading to confusion, but rather actively engaging reality/as Maya.[9]

Bernstein's sense of the 'idea' as being the shape and reverberation, the formal configuration of the 'book,' is a variation and contrast to the characteristics of Alice Notley's *Margaret and Dusty*.[10] The internal workings of her 'book' in its process as if using itself up or being the same as its material are the actual rendition and sound of that music.

A manifestation of postmodernism: the proliferation of the particular—has to do with recognizing social definitions ("The composition is the thing seen by every one living in the living they are doing") as not intrinsic to reality or oneself.

Margaret and Dusty is composed of discrete poems, which are an interwoven pattern of voices and characters. Real individuals sometimes mentioned or addressed by name enter the conversation; people are quoted and designated by name as in "Bob & Simon's Waltz"; unnamed multiple voices interweave snatches of conversation; imaginary characters address each other as in the piece "Postcards"; a poem may be entirely a monologue by some other character as in "At The End-Of-School Party"; or the author carries on conversations with invisible presences, reading aloud from a book or newspaper or responding off-the-cuff to TV or movies as part of the conversation.

Parts of poems are designated as songs. The songs are formal variations and projections of the particular poem in which they're found.

The authorial voice in a chatty, daffy duration of a sort of "Macho Daisy Duck" (a poem in which she titles her own voice) becomes apparent as a social surface, or a constructed personality.

The subject of one's 'life' is discussed in terms of the conventional conception of the separation of autobiography from the 'book.' This subject also relates to actual life and death—i.e., the separation of life from 'book' is narrowed or erased—by the fact of the author dealing with the occurrence of an actual death, thus going past the confines of the book. Social construction and private experience of reality are seen as the same, mirrored in each other:

> I learned two things from the play last night,
> God is Love, & when you're dead you're dead.

[9] *Maya*, reality as infinite multiplicities of illusion.
[10] Alice Notley, *Margaret & Dusty* (St. Paul, Minn., 1985).

Look at this picture, that was his look that when
he looked at you like that you felt terrific.
I'll never get to see him again.
What's it like out?

The creation of the voices in *Margaret and Dusty* apes projections of
what we think 'life' is, or what we think ourselves are. People are
mimicked to be seen as social configurations and also as "talk," the
conversations in the book which are the abstraction the only existence of
the person. I.e., the poem or projections of the person are the news or
conversations:

Gloria Steinem will speak at length on abortion.
Can I have 35¢ for baseball cards?
I just want to be in my life!
Where are you?
In my life!
I am a black lace fan.
I need the paper & the many little mineral waters.
Unacceptable to Winfield & Jackson.

Stock maxims, understood in the poem as socially derived sentiment,
occur as overtly imposed or mimicked voices—therefore the reader comes
to a view of sentiment, and to an accuracy in experience of a sentiment,
which is different from the stereotype.
As in Cindy Sherman's use of costume, the seeing of oneself as social
form a kind of hyped Presence, causes oneself to open up and fly apart.

All things belie me, I think, but I
look at them though. Well boys, at
least you're not dead, right? What's
the date today? Until something. What?
Of the lady of the whitening blow.
I'm ashamed to keep on babbling
as if I've always been oneself,
diamond flow through. Humble
flannel skeleton. Grin, laugh unbecoming
Living at the bottom of the water may

36

have been obvious all the time. But
I forget. What's my plot? Hand
of a child, paw of an animal.

The sense of time in this book is a phase of intense emotion. The process of the 'book' is that of using itself up; the conversation of all those people in the writing becomes the only stuff there is:

what would you think then? But I
wouldn't do that. Light surrounded oranges
towels clouds. You don't think you're my you.
Not here not you. You still think you're he. she.
Because I wouldn't "you" you, would I? I only
"you" some other he. she. I
who writes poems. When she writes them,
it's different...

The author in the 'book' is just that person, which is simply and purely the created other characters, such as Margaret and Dusty.

Sweet, a play

SWEET
A PLAY

Performed by four or five people,
who speak poems or share parts of
poems. The set is the curb of a
street. There is a park bench on
a sidewalk. The back wall, or all
three walls, have a scene being
shown from a movie projector of
ocean waves filmed coming in to
the shore and sometimes reversed
so that the viewer is in the midst
of the ocean watching the waves go
to the shore.

the light fleet that's attacking them—meeting them, as they're coming
there to attack—can move, the dark squall coming up in the sky, and the
Spanish Armada lolling heavily cannot maneuver drift in the (other) fleet
coming in and out

journalist as caught and made to confess
by terrorists, bound by them—seen in front of everyone
on film—and gets away from them—as
just amazing, him on film too then
as was the other

> revolting
> rebelling—gone—though
> of—ever—imagining that—or
> ever having wanted that—or known it
> from—someone

so scene of
looming figure—with red long faked
sensual
tongue—in foreground—on sand of
small faked people—as if ant eater in obviously
just—only—visual—we're

the journalist
has genuinely escaped
on his own
from the terrorists—and
returns

---

arabian nights like—scene—of
many scenes—with—skittering figure
in minor erotic
escapades—mild—dabbling as really
—revolting—erotica

"revolting" is

said

getting

by others

past walls into purdah—scene—of
many scenes—and on sand in
arabian nights like—so skittering
revolting
figure—roles—in
—and therefore erotic—plural

so looming ant eater figure—on foreground
of—sand people small faked—as same
journalist
escaped—as when he was captured and also then
seen by everyone—on film

the
walk
out—shops and to
coffee shops passersby
there—but just there
only in the scene
which is there

       to have
       wandered in a deep
       depression or
       crisis
       though returning from a small thing, conversation
       with someone not known well—out
       —walking
       back
       to have read, by
       sitting down—out—on the curb to relieve being in
       the depression

––––––––––––––––––––

this was some
time ago
—as a young
woman

a passerby
looking with sympathy at a person sitting down, on
the street curb—though that doesn't matter—out
—their having wandered
in a deep depression and
not being able to leave there
—coming there
and walking, reading sitting on the curb—bursting in
the chest—something
—there

relieved—hours—so that
person
having wandered
—unable to return—light
as a feather
returns
walks home

though
being—in
the depression unrelated
to—such

thinking it's
real
that of
—people—died—crowds in
Mecca•riot

where
those from Iran wanting to administer the shrines and having
a demonstration in the midst of Mecca in which the Saudi's to
keep order—in the mass—the sides firing, and a thousand
were killed, as a stream

film showing
samurai are in pampas grass, having
fallen, wounded from fleeing horsemen—in war, but sea
of grass with only them there—and the two
are murdered
by spear piercing them coming through sea
of grass from two peasant women scavengers

      murdered
      samurai are stripped to loin clothes and
      dragged through sea of pampas grass by
      two peasant women scavengers—who—would
      starve—only occurring in the pampas, higher than them—
      the samurai thrown down hole
      in grass

the hole—where dead samurai are thrown by peasants—
seems endless—but only sea of pampas
grass around—outside war, people starving—and
a few
samurai come into grass

      couple—young, adult peasants
      copulating, having to defy old peasant woman in
      pampas grass—who—would
      starve, without the girl—girl and man who're young so access
      to copulating—only—in pampas grass sea where they
      live

going to
places good day
and warm and
without
something that's bothering
anyone—and is
seen

———————————

feeling
misery—in
situation
only
with people who are groupies in
social—as
running astray—or deeply
repressed—scene

     that there's no one
     there except
     the
     groupies in
     their own
     scene—so there is extreme
     loneliness—as that is deeply repressed

there
will never be people
who're
or—not the groupies in
social—scene—as—will ever
be that—in deeply repressed fashion
and circumstance

so we're
not going
to
get out of that
—fashion or
situation ever

a man—
in some ways he's
remarkably free
of being repressed
—very
gentle—muscular—in a deep
serenity
—flesh—and
light bounding

always wanting to be
different from what
one is
—always wanted to be
someone else

———————————————

some people living
less
with a serene
nature
—dying anyway
—though that doesn't matter

       people not wanting to
       have a relation
       to other
       people in close
       way—as
       to that

and
not doing so—having
a relation
close
to anyone—as
in that

or to
do so—
too

white—woman—pale with liquid
blood-colored
interior—seen in her mouth as her figure is lying
on ground—and—pool is seen in
mouth—as scene—only visual

having to be
totally concentrating
which wears one out

---

groupie—but whose fatuous
dominant
because of snobbery—for no reason—
ever—inspiring fury—
and to be concentrating—on him

fatuous—met—snob
from
—(his) small—Indiana view—putrifying
decomposing—condescending with a false
—sense of class—when that's nothing

concentrate—on
this—(to)

---

people, not being able to
work—from just
not wanting to—and decomposing
—bums—flesh—later—and
out, sitting

social life doesn't have anything to do
—with them—people, and so
confusing—for that reason—and getting
out there, sitting

concentrate—only
on—the empty blonde
   candidate
   as being

          I saw
          a prisoner pulling
          flowers or weeds
          by the path
          —and he was on
          a ball-and-chain
          fastened to his
          leg

near-by the prisoner pulling plants on the path, a fenced pen of mired bog
with muddy pigs immersed in it—the small dark pigs floating immersed
up to their sides. I stood by the pen.

to get out of that way of thinking that the pilgrims caught in the street the
crush in Mecca killed were in a stream

          people imitating something but as
          the event,
          the same as—this—action—though it is
          not them—not their actions

the groupies releasing something—gently
turned in on themselves
          or
          not imitating something, and
          it is just up to the surface

the inflated mattress raft of rubber—being
flat on the floor—waking at night—crossed by the
huge roaches which are on one—and so taking turns
sitting in a sink—or hunched on a chair
with the other child—until dawn

deep red sunset
—called to see it—
from the side of the ship
in the ocean

a person
walking—by shops, others—when a man running
then knocks her down—and runs on
with the passerby left there on the sidewalk
—lying, though he turns to see her

that person who was lying running
by a forest, and by ditches
in the afternoon and at dusk and the frogs
croaking at once when she's running
by dusk and evening

in a boat floating—and a
blue
and greenish—dog—swelled belly
so that it was huge—wavered on the shore
—and being in the boat rowing

the corpse wavers
on the shore
comes up to it
touching it—and
being in the boat rowing
further off

the herd
of camels who were dying
of thirst being driven
on to dry wells in the
desert giving their cry of thirst
—traveling under the moon

                    a sack of
                 a baby falls out of a
                 —blood from her rear
      camel—dropping from her dead, on the drive in which
                 the herd is dying of thirst
              traveling fast at night under the moon
                      who're
                 pushed until it's dawn
                      there

            being in an inner-tube floating on
        the lake
            and—isolated, alone there, in the lake in
      the afternoons—and at dusk and at
        dawn being in the boat rowing

Re-living

Egypt is the act of love, in *Helen in Egypt*. It is being dead, so time values are altered. Present is past, past is future: "The whole heroic sequence is over, forgotten, re-lived, forgotten." Achilles, in life, is immortal; after death he's left with only the Achilles-heel. The soul was in life, in the past—which is now the future. The body exists in death:

> it was God's plan
> to melt the icy fortress of the soul,
> and free the man

Achilles is Osiris, Proteus, Dis. He's the ice-star. Paris, who's Helen's lover prior to Achilles, is Eros, Dionysius, the child of Helen and Achilles. The first lover having been created by the last lover. Spring is always in the past. Achilles keeping Helen in the past, obliterates time—so it's the present:

> can spring defeat winter? never,
> spring may come after,
>
> but the crystal, the center, the ice-star
> dissembles, reflects the past
> but waits faithful
> •••
> Paris will never find me;
> I reflect, I re-act, I re-live...

The question is asked, "Is the disguise of death, love...are we home-sick for what has been?" Love is in the past, just as spring is. The scattered dead Greek heroes are the Egyptian flower, also the limbs of Osiris. The thousand-petalled lily is a hieroglyph repeated endlessly so time stops in it. Postulates or pictures are projected from a single reality. The writing is expressed in things: "The secret of the stone-writing is repeated in natural or human symbols. She herself is the writing." People are more than one symbol.

So the pattern can't be "read" or deciphered completely, but only expressed in statements which are declarations of relationships between things. The most abstruse hieroglyphs are the most simple memories, so seeing is in terms of surfaces. Certain sights or pictures through their lines are direct entrances to vision which occurs in over-mind consciousness. In *Thought and Vision*, H.D. says da Vinci for example "saw the faces of many of his youths and babies and young women definitely with his over-mind. The Madonna of the Rocks is not a picture. It is a window. We look through a window into the world of pure over-mind."

The over-mind is a lens, really two. The center of consciousness is either the intellect, which is in Greece—or the love-region of the body, in Egypt. The two lenses work separately, "perceive separately, yet make one picture." The dream as delirium/trance/ecstacy, Helen in Egypt and Helen in Leuké is the sub-conscious world: "The subconscious world is the world of sleeping dreams and the world great lovers enter, physical lovers, but very great ones." The state of being awake and seeing clearly, remembering and not remembering is the waking dream: "The over-conscious world is the world of waking dreams and the world great lovers enter, spiritual lovers, but only the greatest." Helen's soul is snatched from its body—with its body—by the gerfalcon Archilles.

Theseus is Freud, who's to "teach me to remember...teach me not to remember," which is the state of the waking dream. Intellect being the bridge between sub-conscious and over-conscious mind which looks back on thoughts: "Into that over-mind, thoughts pass and are visible like fish swimming under clear water."

Helen's the hollow shell, death/Leuké/mind. Having found or being found by Dis. She's inside the egg-shell, in Hades. The dead Greek heroes are "as one soul, one pearl" asleep in the shell. Re-living, being in time, in thought, reduces time to a finite moment in which there's "all song forever." "There is only a song now and rhetorical questions that have been already answered. The song is the frieze." The song's in herself (in the shell/the mind/ the writing) and the sea enchantment.

So only being in the waking state will free her from enchantment. Paris before and after Egypt is Eros so there's only the present:

> there is no before and no after,
> there is one finite moment
> that no infinite joy can disperse

or though of past happiness
tempt from or dissipate;
now I know the best and the worst...

The world of death is the highest life. Only Dis/Achilles (he's in the past and therefore future time) can break his heart and the world for a token, "a memory forgotten." Which means remembering and forgetting at the same time, the waking day dream or window. In terms of the song, it's "a rhythm as yet unheard."

Things and people being translations, they are lacquered, frozen. In *Hermetic Definition*, she gives birth to Dis at the end of her life; though he's said to be Osiris/Paris/Perseus. He'd died, was much younger than she, so it's seasonal. The rose unfolds through her, unfolding to an impossible degree:

no, no, this is too much,
we can not escape to a new continent;
the middle door is judgement,

I am judged—prisoner?
the reddest rose unfolds,
can I endure this?

There are other roses. The rose that's reddest is therefore formal and external. So it's frenzied, finding in itself "the exact intellectual component/ or the exact emotional opposite." The lover/opposite is perfect. Permitting her to be nothing, to be dead. The writing therefore far away, outside oneself. Re-living is out-living:

and you draw me out
to compete with your frenzy;
there are other roses

H.D., *Notes on Thought and Vision* (San Francisco: City Lights, 1982); *Hermetic Definition* (New York: New Directions, 1972); *Helen in Egypt* (New York: New Directions, 1961).

57

Poetic Diaries

In considering forms of poetic diaries in terms of fictional modes, I'm comparing several Japanese poetic diaries, several modern examples, and two fictional works, primarily Murasaki Shikibu's *The Tale of Genji*. The narrator and other identities in the fiction or in the poetic diary occur only in terms of location and periods of time.

Using for a moment John Thorpe's notion of people and places as being bardo realms, the word "bardo" means "between two." The two are death and rebirth; there is a state or life lived between: "A western analogy might be seen in the *Odyssey*, where Odysseus is going from Troy to Ithaka and keeps being arrested in all these locations along the way."

Odysseus is only himself by being narrated through the bardo realms, always "inhabiting a set which is the poem's present." This conception seems more active in the sense of forward moving than Proust's, say. Proust composing a self by inhabiting detached locations and moments—in a way passively—which in being brought forward are still isolated from each other:

> A piece of landscape brought to the shore of today, 'detaches itself so completely from everything, that it floats uncertain in my thought like a flowering Delos, without my being able to say from what country, from what time—perhaps, very simply, from what dream—it comes.'

The diary of Izumi Shikibu, for example, isn't her life. It covers a brief, specified period of time. The courtship and early phase of a love affair between Izumi Shikibu and a certain prince, culminating in her removal from her own house and placement in his. This resulting in her transplanting the principle wife, who leaves feeling humiliated by the presence of the concubine—so close at hand and of a lower rank.

The diary is in the third person; so she's describing herself and her lover, their feelings in exchanges of poems, their conversations—from a point of view which an outsider could not know. The narrator describes herself—in terms of internal states, from outside that time. Also implies or enters internal states felt by the principle wife before that wife's departure. The diary concluding with the thought "What has been given above is not the wording of the letter of the Prince's Consort or of what was spoken by the ladies in the palace; it is rather what the author has imagined. So my manuscript says."

The Confessions of Lady Nijo is written as the sequence of her life; the first event is her betrothal at the age of fourteen to the retired emperor, who's admitted to her room one night without her having been told of the marriage. Intensity occurs as a result of seeing outside states of time. He's unable to persuade her on that first night. The time span of the second night is recorded after he forces her, which occurs in the diary in one sentence:

Tonight, when GoFukakusa could not elicit a single word of reply from me, he treated me so mercilessly that my thin gowns were badly ripped. By the time that I had nothing more to lose, I despised my own existence. I faced the dawn with dread.

Ties of my undergowns undone,
The man uncared for—
Gossip soon will spread.

What surprised me, as I continued to brood, was that I still had wits enough to think of my reputation.

GoFukakusa was expressing his fidelity with numerous vows. 'Though from life to life our shapes will change,' he said, 'there will be no change in the bond between us; though the nights we meet might be far apart, our hearts will never acknowledge separation.' As I listened, the short night, barely affording time to dream, gave way to dawn and the tolling of bells. It was past daybreak. 'It will be embarrassing if I stay,' GoFukakusa said, getting up to leave. 'Even if you are not sorry we must part, at least see me off.'

Unable to refuse his insistent urgings, I slipped a thin, unlined gown over the clothes I had on, which were damp from a night of weeping, and stepped outside. The moon of the seventeenth night was sinking in the west, and a narrow bank of clouds stretched along the eastern horizon. GoFukakusa wore a green robe, scarlet-lined, over a pale gown. He had on heavily figured trousers. I felt more attracted to him than I ever had before, and I wondered uneasily where these new feelings had come from.

The states are in the present—and remembered at the same time (the night is the present—it's being over is as well—as is her remembering desiring the man). In the present also in the sense of a strong feeling being expressed in terms of convention (the lover's departure at dawn, the clothes damp from weeping).

The diary ends shortly after an account of Lady Nijo as a middle-aged woman running after the retired emperor's coffin through the streets on the way to the crematory late at night—barefoot because she's lost her shoes. Having been ousted from the court by the empress, his principle wife, many years before at the age of twenty-six, she has been a nun since then, now unable to gain access either to the retired emperor's deathbed or to the room in which his coffin is viewed—since she no longer has any ties in the world.

Having outlived oneself—is a connection to Mallarmé's *A Tomb for Anatole*: his own life is not the subject. It is written in response to the death of his son, a short time encompassed. It's a notational form of a projected work—in which the writing/diary/his life will be his son's. He implies his own death, reversing the order which has occurred in actual life (his son's death having been first) to be the son—in order to extend himself. The basis being that the son's death cuts off the parents' life—if he is the projection:

> child sprung from
> the two of us—showing
> us our ideal, the way
> —our! father
> and mother who
>   sadly existing
> survive him as
> the two extremes—
> badly coupled in him
> and sundered
> —from whence his death—o-
> bliterating this little child "self"

The time frame is for a future—in addition to the father, everyone in the present is sacrificed for the one person. The construction of time becomes visible—since there is no other time frame than that in the poem.

A connection to *The Tales of Ise*—in which a fictional character is created by an unknown author drawn from the poetic diary of the courtier poet Arihara no Narihira. To extend his life—by means of arriving at the idealized mode of that time. The entire subject is the love affairs of the nameless hero[1]—a sequence of narrative and poems which are to each other afterthoughts or forethoughts. There is no plot. Implying that in a

---

[1] So it's the present in terms of convention—the past hero is idealized—and in that he isn't conventional. Arihira no Narihira seen in this time as highly individualistic—for example, he wrote in the Japanese language, while the convention for men was to write in the Chinese characters. (The Heian classics were primarily written by women.)

polygamous society in a period of transition, the relations between the sexes would be limitless (according to H. Jay Harris, the sense of rank was not as fixed then as in the later period in which *The Tale of Genji* was written).

A youth of twelve to fifteen, the hero in the first section peers through a fence and sees two sisters:

> Cutting the cuff from the hunting cloak he was wearing, the young man wrote a poem and sent them in. The young man had on a hunting cloak of the mottled purple Shinobu pattern.
>
> > Fields of Kasuga
> > with whose tender purple shoots
> > this gown has been dyed:
> > This confusion of my heart
> > whose boundaries no man knows...
>
> Thus like a man beyond his years did he compose and send his song.
> And would he not have gradually thought more wonderful things—
>
> > From Michinoku
> > come the patterns of hateweed:
> > Who may be the cause
> > of emotions muddling—
> > I am not the source of this.
>
> Such was his meaning. The men of former times thus felt such deep elegance.

His not being the source of the dye or pattern—yet feeling it.

Not being the source of the pattern—is a tie to Genji.

In terms of Proust: each place revealing itself as the seat of an original reality, having nothing in common with other places, even with those that adjoin it—everything is in the past—this implies an active construction of one's life in a way. The Heian world as a flowering Delos—as fiction. The mansion is a maze of detached pavilions and connecting galleries open to the outside. So there isn't any privacy—also this is the only world, being the court, and insulated; so though people age and die—it is present time always. Constitutes that world's present—in the midst of which is foresight, or premonition; which could also be a flashback—in a passage—because of the resemblances in events.

> He glanced over toward the Third Princess's rooms. They seemed to be in the usual clutter. The multicolored sleeves pouring from under the blinds

and through openings between them were like an assortment of swatches to be presented to the goddess of spring.[2] Only a few paces from him a woman had pushed her curtains carelessly aside and looked as if she might be in a mood to receive a gentleman's addresses. A Chinese cat, very small and pretty, came running out with a larger cat in pursuit. There was a noisy rustling of silk as several women pushed forward to catch it. On a long cord which had become badly tangled, it would not yet seem to have been fully tamed. As it sought to free itself the cord caught in a curtain, which was pulled back to reveal the woman behind. No one, not even those nearest the veranda, seemed to notice. They were much too worried about the cat.

The passage quoted is a projection outwards, forwards—like 3D—toward the reader; the beginning of a stream of events. Kashiwagi falling in love with the Third Princess after seeing her in this scene, though he's described as having been ready to fall in love—leading to his taking her against her will, afterwards dreaming of a cat, which is conception, though he does not know why he's had the dream; she has in face conceived—is one of Genji's wives—the reaction (as if it were outside her) is becoming a nun, Kashiwagi's death in remorse, lack of self-knowledge. His weakness of character is revealed—not in his seducing her—but as having been there already.

Foresight—in terms of a narrative device—is not determinism. There is an understanding of what someone is in the present—they later turn out to be that; the understanding and their character/actions simply have deepened. They have become more themselves, are revealed to themselves.

Similar to Genji's visiting each lady singly, their becoming known to him—the ladies are living in the present with the lotuses opening behind them in the past.

In all the other quarters, there were only distant echoes of horse and carriage, to make the ladies feel that they were living in an outer circle of paradise where the lotuses were slow to open.

Some of them old, some relationships never having been consummated—there are no screens or curtains to inhibit him—so the outer and inner world are the same. (A premonition of stagnation—in terms of rank.

[2] Women remained behind curtains or screens, and traveled in closed carriages. Merely catching sight of a woman would be the impetus for a love affair with her.

Again, love affairs carried on either in secret or in public being the means of transition.)

Genji remembers everything; but some of the women being neglected, there's movement at the outer edges, or in the middle or center, unknown to him; i.e., really there aren't outer edges in the frame. John Thorpe's notion:

> So a lot of obtuse stresses produce a fragmentary utterance, and if it accumulates I have to face it one way or another or I'm just going to spin out of the date....For me the way out of this dilemma isn't to think in terms of beginnings and ends, but of *middles* which open and close the set.

> She spoke in a tiny, wavering voice and she was like a beautiful child. He hurried out as if he had only half heard, and felt as if he were leaving his soul behind.

> In my thought, a rose is not object for poetry but as a co-poet, both as signified and signifier.

Wandering is what Genji is in terms of the lady of the locust shell—because it is not consummated. The passages, widely separated, in which she occurs are therefore fast time. In one passage, he enters her rooms, guided by her small brother. She flees in the darkness leaving her companion, who's asleep. The other woman wakes. He makes love with her. Leaving, he picks up a robe dropped by the first lady—and later broods on her fragrance which lingers in the robe:

> Beneath a tree, a locust's empty shell.
> Sadly I muse upon the shell of a lady.

It's not being consummated is a middle ground—leaving an opening. Nothing occurring once he'd gotten past the curtains to her, regardless of consummating it with anyone else there.

Therefore in terms of time, a budless spring—which is really lush as if it were flowering—indicative of the narrator moving away from or out of the frame or set, leaving it behind. Genji'd taken the robe in the past, later the lady's seen in his keeping, as a nun—so it's too late to consummate it at that date. This is fast time in the sense of Genji seeing her completely—seeing her lifetime, obviously an intrusive observation on the part of the narrator. The lady says then: "My contrition is in showing myself to you as I am, and in having you see me thus to the end."

Multiple resemblances of people and of events within a set, or widely separated from each other in narrative—and sets which occupy an extended time, opening up and unfolding so that it's the whole world in which things and people move slowly—create the present.

Passages occur in a stream of resemblances. Genji as a youth catches a forbidden glimpse of his father's concubine, Fujitsubo, resulting in a love affair; later he duplicates her in his wife Murasaki, who resembles her. Later still, he forbids his son Yuguri access to or sight of Murasaki; Yuguri sees her, desires her. After Murasaki dies, Genji dies. Kaoru becomes the hero—pursuing one woman in two of her sisters, after the first woman's death.

These interiors created—which isn't determinism—the erotic moment is also the totally open-ended moment. In the following passage the "regained moment," the interior garden—though we are looking back—is actually a moment that's open. The curtains blow open in the interior and Yuguri sees Murasaki and Genji together.

> Yuguri looked back. Smiling at Murasaki, Genji was so young and handsome that Yuguri found it hard to believe he was looking at his own father. Murasaki too was at her best. Nowhere could there be a nearer approach to perfection than the two of them, thought Yuguri, with a stabbing thrill of pleasure. The wind had blown open the shutters along the gallery to make him feel rather exposed. He withdrew. Then, going to the veranda, he coughed as if to announce that he had just arrived.
>
> "See," said Genji, pointing to the open door. "You have been quite naked."
>
> Nothing of the sort had been permitted through all the years. Wind can move boulders and they had reduced the careful order to disarray, and so permitted the remarkable pleasure that had just been Yuguri's.

The son looking at the father and wife—in their youth—so it's really a moment that could not and has never occurred. It is therefore outside of memory.

Revelation of character in innuendo—a middle ground created in that—would be limitless in terms of meaning and interpretation.

Ivan Morris comments that a literal translation of Heian language results in a floating, diffuse structure in which neither speakers nor those performing an action are specifically differentiated. A diffuseness or lack of accuracy, which is increased by the repetition of the same emotive words, whose range of meaning is multiple.

For people who live in a small, closed society, like that of the Heian court, the entire range of experience will be so familiar that the briefest hint will suffice to convey one's meaning, and any systematic exposition of one's thoughts is regarded as otiose, even boorish. Language becomes a sort of shorthand, immediately understood by those who are 'in,' vague and slightly mysterious to the outsider.

The Tale of Genji was read to the court, including the emperor. It took twenty years to compose. So it existed as spoken—as a social occurrence.

Though not the reigning beauty of the day, this other daughter had elegance and dignity and a pleasantly gentle manner. She was like a plum blossom opening at dawn. Her father loved the way she had of making it seem that a great deal was being left unsaid.

She's totally exposed—as the plum blossom opening at dawn. And the frames (of what is being left unsaid) in so far as they create a location as yet unknown—create a world that has not been there before.

Kaoru's character is seen to have "limitless depths"—and he is exposed to others and brings out his surrounding by his fragrance, which emanates from his body. The depths therefore in a frame are multiple. The notion is of passages in which character or settings become locations of nothing known.

This was not the sort of journey he was accustomed to. It was sobering and at the same time exciting.
From leaves that cannot withstand the mountain wind
The dew is falling. My tears fall yet more freely.
He forbade his outrunners to raise their cries, for the woodcutters in these mountains could be troublesome. Brushing through a wattle fence, crossing a rivulet that meandered down from nowhere, he tried as best he could to silence the hoofs of his colt. But he could not keep that extraordinary fragrance from wandering off on the wind, and more than one family awoke in surprise at 'the scent of an unknown master.'

The person not being known—to themselves or others—and being reordered or disordered by a strong emotion. (So it's a sort of middle ground).

The lady of the Gossamer Diary (a generation before *Genji*) rejecting the romances of the period in favor of writing a "life"—which is seen as states of reaction to her husband (who had eight or nine wives or concubines) over twenty or so years, though the diary is written in a condensed period of time. Her desire for a monogamous marriage would have been and was considered to be unreasonable. Her relationships with everyone around her become increasingly more dislocated.

> All through the Twenty-fourth a gentle rain was falling. Toward evening I had an odd letter from him: "I have been put off by your fearsome antics and have stayed away these many days." I did not answer.
> The rain continued the following day, but my tears proposed to outlast it. As I sat looking out I thought of the poem about retreating from the world when the joy of spring is at its height. "These thoughts torment me in infinite detail," I recited to myself, "and my tears fall as the drops of rain...."
> On about the twentieth day of the retreat I dreamed that my hair was cut and my forehead bared like a nun. Seven or eight days later I dreamed that a viper was crawling among my entrails and gnawing at my liver, and that the proper remedy for the difficulty was to pour water over my face. I do not know whether these dreams were good or bad, but I write them down so that those who hear of my fate will know what trust to put in dreams and signs from the Buddha.
> Early in the Fifth Month I had a note from the people at my house asking whether they should put out irises even though I was not at home. Not to do so, they thought, might be bad luck. I wondered what difference it could possibly make and jotted down a verse: "I have grown away from the world—what have these irises to do with me?" I wanted to send it to them, but I knew that they would not understand.

States of dislocation are objectified—given duration—so they have a life of their own. We're to accept the terms of those states—in order to compare them to convention.

A tie to Clark Coolidge's *Mine: The One That Enters the Stories.* Repetition of statements creating frames—in which everything is to be given equal value, thereby exposing itself.

> The prime nature of the question is a repetition that, through saturation and standing wave duration, eventually results in statement. Next to the list was tacked a manuscript casting a fictional light on the origin of the square in a fictional light.

The writing/dislocations in it is a fiction of oneself.[3] Fiction leading to a premonition of stagnation. Thought and action are the same. Therefore

---

[3] which are resemblances, internal rhymes—or songs.

plots are the past—"Celia's thought of a beach."

We're turned into outsiders. "Some events have no semblance at all in the mind. They strictly occur"—duration in the work is to eliminate so as to create frames which are locations of nothing known.

> But does the story move out, as of a house to where. In the story he told he lived on the second floor. But narrative does not (easily?) possess an ascendancy. He wanted to walk down the street. He wished to walk backwards all of his further life and never be told of his act and to continue seeing the glaring world fleeing from his reach.
>
> He walked backwards down the avenue with nothing on his mind. Never again would he worry past windows, conceive of any passing body a threatener. He could have been waltzing for all that passed him by. His reflection led him out of danger. Facades seemed to float in rhyme with the chunks of metal hurtling past on this calm afternoon. He had left it all behind, for the moment at least glorious in thoughtless but visible retreat.
>
> He was cool. His mind had tamed. No one could see him. He began to reorganize the city.
>
> I want to leave these fixed words and enter the dagger cities.

The notion of a world "beyond the mind" is projected in the future as a thought—"Everyone involved in the outermost ways has forgotten to care about the contents of the room. They walk about in a wind of their own deed." (The deed, the action being in the past.)

There aren't other people.

"Celia's thought of a beach." A variation on this and also a contrast: the notion of there not being identity except as events and in events. All events are in the past—and I was seen then and only see in the present in terms of other people and the social world.

Therefore my thought, and events which are outside me—and really are me—and the world, are the same. Very painful events may seem to have longer reverberations. Which cause their own reordering. This implies a syntax which in being read would require that the reader go through the process of its thought, have that thought again—and it's therefore an act, one which has not occurred before. A thought of the writer isn't going to be duplicated.

A connection to this is Laurie Anderson's poetic diary in the form of documentation of acts as portraits of others. She's merely seen—in that there are photographs of her, along with the stories.

The diary form is a documentation of a performance which occurred at particular locations and times. "This is the time. And this is the record of the time."

Duets on Ice: was performed at five locations—played on a violin which had a built-in speaker, that is, a self-playing violin. Half the duet was on tape coming out of the violin and the other half was played, simultaneously, live. The timing mechanism was the skates I wore, their blades frozen into blocks of ice. When the ice melted the concert was over. Between songs I talked about the parallels. In awkward Italian, I told a group of people at the Porta Soprana in Genoa that I was playing these songs in memory of my grandmother because the day she died I went out for a walk on a frozen lake and saw a flock of ducks honking and flapping their wings. I got very close to them but they didn't fly away. Then I saw their feet had frozen into the new layer of ice. One man who heard me tell this story was explaining to newcomers, "She's playing these songs because once she and her grandmother were frozen together into a lake.'

Also, obviously since the act is a duet—using a self-playing violin—it incorporates a previous act.

Works Cited

Anderson, Laurie. Exhibitions at UCLA, Los Angeles.

Brazell, Karen, trans. *The Confessions of Lady Nijo*. Stanford, Calif.: Stanford University Press, 1973.

Coolidge, Clark. *Mine: The One That Enters the Stories*. Berkeley, Calif.: The Figures, 1982.

Harris, H. Jay, trans. *The Tales of Ise*. Tokyo: Charles E. Tuttle Co., 1972.

Mallarmé, Stephane, *A Tomb for Anatole*. Trans. Paul Auster. Berkeley: North Point Press, 1983.

Miner, Earl, trans. *Japanese Poetic Diaries*. Berkeley: University of California Press, 1969.

Morris, Ivan, *The World of the Shining Prince: Court Life in Ancient Japan*. Tokyo: Charles E. Tuttle Co., 1978.

Poulet, Georges, *Proustian Space*. Trans. Elliott Coleman, Baltimore: Johns Hopkins University Press, 1977.

Seidensticker, Edward G., trans. *The Gossamer Years (Kagero Nikki): The Diary of a Noblewoman of Heian Japan.* Tokyo: Charles E. Tuttle Co., 1969.

Shikibu, Murasaki. *The Tale of Genji.* Trans. Edward G. Seidensticker, New York: Alfred A. Knopf, 1982.

Thorpe, John. *Poetry as Air Traffic Control.* Bolinas: Smithereens Press, 1984.

fin de siècle, 20th
a play

FIN DE SIÈCLE, 20th
A PLAY

The poems are spoken modestly and melodiously by a man (1) and woman (2) surrounded by a backdrop of a vast savanna. In the distance are scattered hanging frames (abstract sculptures) of cars.

1. went into a camp
    in the desert and they were sitting
    around a fire out there at night

                    no person
                    from there
         2. is present in the ordering
              of the siege
              of their capital

                              war which our country
                              directs and the other foreign
                              capital wanting their capital to fall
                              from their rebels

the newspaper says
what is a newspaper
what are who creating this
being
or are in this

                    Chaucer, he knew
         1. *spring*
              he had spring down

                    The army withdrawing—of the Soviets—and into
                    the fragile construction—there—conceived
                    from a foreign capital—is a seige—which flimsy
                    does not collapse their structure

and the prime minister
of the foreign capital
says we are troubled by refugees
but they have a war there

her ministers of the foreign capital
deciding against the siege
2. and the seige was ordered from there
being
of the other's rebels on their capital

Not seeing this or remembering as it is real

people speaking

when you speak of
1. people on the street
I am that

he says and he was
in the war

2. narration of their construction is
fragile—being

they were hearing my reading and
a woman with child—going into
labor, it was going to be born

the land is thin
as—without
—the war

newspaper boy has maroon fingernails
1. at stand and man makes fun of him
but he's dying and does, collapsing

the maroon fingernails
are a symptom which other
dying victims have

virtual doctrine of
us and the foreign capital
is that the other capital will fall

2. early/from
the rebels

1. early on in them
or out in they

2. if it does not fall soon
what will become of them

man in—fragile
1. capital
hamburger stands strip

it is just merely only beautiful
or just only ugly

just reading

the newspaper says
2. inner chief gains in
portraying their rebels
as foreign tools

we are not that
that's not what is meant

we are thin putting things
1. on the earth not digging and so
innocent and hopeful

2. I wrote this and then
I fell asleep

woke up in the morning

        I'm willingly in
        the lowly horde

carts cars going by
clogged
I took a shower in a dream

               I
               got into the shower stand
               stall in a place I'd
               come in

        being thin from the land or
        not putting thing on it and
        technology though as flat
        being
        rather than people in it   so
                                     our—not
                                     creating it

is
not seeing this or remembering
and so is—that
and is the land

fin de siècle, III
a play

FIN DE SIÈCLE, III
A PLAY

Done in a soft manner by two women who stand separated from each other in a long space, one set a ways back from the other. They use microphones on poles, speaking enunciating slowly with pauses after the poems as from a well or large field. Three of the poems are sung in a melodious soprano and contralto. A few sounds of reed instruments are heard beginning at the second "pause."

1. at night stream-
ing like rats

                crowds of millions tearing at Khomeini's
                corpse for scraps of the shroud
                carrying it trampling screaming trampled
                swaying fealty

                                in the street at night
                                to stop the tanks

       stopped them sometimes
2.   pulling people out of the trucks
       and rejoiced

                    innocent
                    longing

      1.   soldiers lost in the park

firing of the soldiers who're
from the countryside who do
who'll
shoot them freely

             2.   they do
                firing

81

man with bird cage up to tanks
says to the soldiers they're animals and
they shoot him in the chest murdering him

soldiers in streets in trucks
down streets
1. who're chanting
down with chaos
down with chaos

                        the tanks come
                        through and crush over people
            2. and firing lines
                        some climb into crevices and are
                        pulled down within range

            the old men who
        1. order this wanting
            fealty from them

                        octogenarian military men
                        sitting at a table praising the army
                        for the massacre after

dictator's military hand in their civil
war ours is supporting is
2. gunned down
and our official says I am shocked at
the gunning down of
a 73-year-old man

                    I always thought one had to be tough
            1. I like the lowly
                    because they are tough

        long time when
        there's not saying
        of anything just swimming
        and walking

(pause)

we looked down
from the roof of the capital on
2.   mass of chanting
flocking people up the street
in the moist air

                      he's depressed that we're who're
                      who'll
                      here in the air attacking what is "for
                      the people"

                                    we say

———————————————

(pause)

you know people through
time and they don't value anyone
1. and hurt and can't redeem themselves
and don't realize that

                drunks

             2.   the bureaucrats
         (sung as if   on the roof
         a Provençal   drinking
         love song)   in the sweltering dusk
                        of the city

          wind wheeling on the pond surface
   1.   while man in rags paces behind park bench
 (sung) back and forth
          back and forth

                           seen under clump of trees

(sung)   hanging over bench
                           back and forth
                           back and forth

the proposition:

      people here are stopping
2.   people on the street
      women stopping men

                  red
                  poppy fields huge
                  heavy drooping swept
                  in the wind

                        row houses and
                        the families're out on their stoops
                        in the heat

             just go through the city
1.   and go into any house
             throws open the door—they don't
             mind

                    they're fourteen in
                    a room

ducks come down
on the pond surface couples
strolling on the other side in
dispersed formation

                  2.   that is
                       random

                                        beating sun
                                        beating
                                        beating

(she runs loping in
a loop several times
slowly forward and then
returning to her place)

                                              not quite right

                    (she turns
                    in a circle)   not quite right

                                              not quite right

            just sitting on a bench
            of the dispersed
            benches

                                    drank some liquid
                                    sitting
                                    bowed under the
                                    slight shade

the people were out.
the liquid.
some
drank

                        then and forward
                        runs
                        slowly

                                        rubbing

                                85

shade slight
the under bowed
sitting
liquid some drank

                    as no anxiety
                    as
                    to that

Murasaki Duncan

MURASAKI DUNCAN

Robert Duncan gave a talk which I attended at the New College (it was probably in 1981) on Murasaki Shikibu's *The Tale of Genji*. I would like to use Murasaki as a juxtaposition and comparison (the juxtaposition is my own; it is not Duncan's words about Murasaki) to consider a few aspects of Duncan's views of myth and the story. I'll refer to his essay "The Truth and Life of Myth."

Duncan described Jess and himself reading the 10th Century Japanese novel aloud to each other, referred to it as the text of love, and in his talk interwove his comments about the text with digressions about meeting and being in love with Jess.

In his essay on myth, Duncan describes having been raised on and 'formed' by the series he read as a child, the twelve volume *My Book House* edited by Mrs. Olive Beapuré Miller. I also was raised and 'formed' by *My Book House*. This was a collection of nursery rimes, tales, poems, myths drawn from Shakespeare, Dante, and from Greek, Japanese, European, Navajo, and other sources. The connection and juxtaposition in the editor's arrangement of the stories was as important in forming a meaning as was their content and the accompanying pictures.

Duncan mentions *My Book House*, his associations arising from these books, "to give some idea of how little a matter of 'free' association and how much a matter of an enduring design in which the actual living consciousness arises, how much a matter of actual times and actual objects the living reality of the myth is for the poet."

He's defining myth in the essay as one's experience, but that as *experience imagined*: "May there not be a hint that what we experience in our actual life is also what has entered the imagination and there been imagined as experience?"

> In Goya's canvas Cupid and Psyche
> have a hurt voluptuous grace
> bruised by redemption. The copper light
> falling upon the brown boy's slight body
> is carnal fate that sends the soul wailing
> up from blind innocence, ensnared
> by dimness
> into the deprivations of desiring sight

Duncan is examining in "A Poem Beginning With A Line By Pindar" the myth of Cupid and Psyche through the interpretation of it by Goya's canvas and by the Christian myth of the Fall. "Carnal fate" is the copper light in the painting falling upon the boy. The light comes from outside. The conception of "carnal fate" is also implied by both myths; Duncan evokes our prior knowledge as experience of passion, via the myths as well as the poet's own implicit inner identification with it (the concept of carnal fate).

He is investigating fiction, as well as historical event, as an emanation of the psyche.

The Tale of Genji is the *place* of the Heian court. It is the actual world of that time. The form of Murasaki's work which is a vast extension modulated as a subtle sound pattern with over a thousand short poems, is architecturally the maze of detached pavilions and connecting galleries separated by screens which is the Heian world.

Heian Japanese had fewer words than modern Japanese. This was before the incorporation of many Chinese characters. Repetition of the same emotive words whose range of meaning is multiple, resulted in a floating, diffuse structure in which neither speakers nor those performing an action are specifically differentiated. There is not the isolated individual. The women remained behind curtains or screens, traveled in closed carriages; they passed poems under the screens which were set up in public gatherings. Everyone communicated by poems; functions of state and courtships were furthered taking place by exchange of poems.

As content: extension of relationships (both between people, and in nuance of meaning—which is shared references possible in such an insulated world) which is implicitly infinite.

Compare to Duncan's view of myth as the grammar of rimes.

The Tale of Genji was read to the court, including the emperor. It was written over a period of twenty years. So it existed primarily as spoken, as a social occurrence. It would have been regarded as totally in present time. Being that life (of the court). It views passion and the beauty of the world and as such reflects the Buddhist conception of time and reality as empty or Void.

An example of the emptiness of self or identity is the "empty shell" of the locust lady who appears in two widely separated brief passages in the novel. In the first passage, Genji enters the lady's rooms at night guided by her small brother. She flees in the darkness leaving her robe and a lady companion, who's asleep. The other woman wakes. He makes love with her; and later broods on the first lady's fragrance which lingers in the robe:

> Beneath a tree, a locust's empty shell.
> Sadly I muse upon the shell of a lady.

Later the locust lady is seen in his keeping as a nun, their relationship not consummated—so he sees her completely in the sense of seeing her lifetime, which is now over (because she is a nun). Seeing someone completely is to see the "empty shell."

Genji himself exists only in relation to other people.

Reality as void—as the Buddhist conception—was part of the communal knowledge of Heian culture.

compare to Duncan's comment in regard to demythologizing that "We have voided the *material* world, as well as God."

Walter Benjamin, in his essay "The Storyteller," describes the art of storytelling as active in that the mode of Homer or other storytellers is to transmit experience, which by being free of explanation in the form of psychological or other connection, enables the listener to integrate this as his own experience. According to Benjamin, the art of the storyteller has declined, a process beginning with World War I with the advent of modern war, tyranny of the state, and economic contingencies which have devalued experience. The form of storytelling is distinct from the form of information, e.g. the newspaper:

> no event any longer comes to us without already being shot through with explanation. In other words, by now almost nothing that happens benefits storytelling; almost everything benefits information. Actually, it is half the art of storytelling to keep a story free from explanation as one reproduces it...the most extraordinary things, marvelous things, are related with the greatest accuracy, but the psychological connection of the events is not forced on the reader. It is left up to him to interpret things the way he understands them, and thus the narrative achieves an amplitude that information lacks.

The epic was read aloud to the community. Benjamin makes a distinction between that active form as storytelling and the 'book' the rise of the novel read by the solitary isolated individual. The solitary individual is uncounselled and cannot counsel others. The form of psychological connection of the novel both reflects and creates this isolation.

Duncan notes in "The Truth and Life of Myth" the demythologizing of education which strips the poet as well as the community of "the common property of man's myths (as) a resource of working material, a grammar of rimes."

He uses the example of the separation of Church and state as a factor in this process. A separation which we accurately identify as democratic, non-authoritarian.

Demythologizing has to do with invalidating experience. Duncan says, "The word 'sentimental' means 'supposed' experience, I suppose."

He links the invalidating by the academic critic of any mythic conception to an implicitly authoritarian stance of invalidating the experience of humble people or the ordinary person.

> The modern mind has not only chickened out on God, on angels, on Creation, but it has chickened out on the common things of our actual world, taking the properties of things as their uses and retracting all sense of fellow creatureliness. Not only the presences of gods and of ideas are denied, becoming for the modern man "supposed" experiences, but the presences of stones, trees, animals and even men as spiritual beings is exorcized in our contemporary common sense. Wherever this contempt moves, it strikes to constrict the realm of empathy. And we see a middle-class meanness of mind that not only rejects from consideration high-flying lordly pretensions—thought that is moved by the grandeur of the universe, time beyond the time of man and space beyond the solar system, the rose of light that Dante in the heights of his vision saw and the remains first in Creation—but likewise dismisses all consideration of spiritual being in humble persons. Man may see by symbols, reading meanings into things and events; much of what he calls experience arises from purely verbal activity. There can be no true significance, no sign that mineral or plant can give in which we have a proper communication, no language whereby things may speak to us. Where the whole field of human experience is man's own, psychology and semantics take over. Signs are no longer presences but poetic sentimentalities, mere fancies, or, wherever men still would speak with the world about them and take the universe into his council, symptoms of psychopathology.

The conception of the 'personal' which is the isolated individual and the 'voiding' of the material world itself are merely corollaries of each other. This is the worker removed from his work:

> It is the very idea that there is a miraculous grace ever about us, a mystery of person, that our modern critic refuses to allow. Personality takes the place of the individual living soul.

And again: "as if wonder came from some power of the writer's and was not a grace recognized by the writer in the reality of things."

Compare to an example of recent writing which analyzes, by reflecting, our current myth, i.e. as that voiced by the newspapers, advertisements, and television. The poems in being the voice of 'media-speak' intend to unravel that social fabrication to get to the center of it. The 'media-speak' is regarded as objectively apparent. Not knowing what we are, we analyze what is 'voicing' us. The poems give up all other ground of observation of people thus seen as clichés. Experience is only the information. There is no 'inner' self or individual, yet the information (the news) is fiction.

The actual media is completely artificial. We are not it. Yet we are trained to regard it as the manifestation of the polis.

The significance of storytelling for Duncan is akin to Benjamin's view in the sense that the poet is in present time in each immediate event of the poem. The following is from "The Truth and Life of Myth:"

> Not only in the symphony, but in the telling of the story and in the composition of the poem, powerful impulses towards pattern emerge along lines of felt relationships and equilibrations having their immediate locus in each immediate event of the poem.

Restoring the sequence of a memory is also in present time and is the process of analyzing the construction of it, as in his having to restore the series of associations which occurred when reading in childhood Mrs. Olive Beapuré Miller's version of Basho and the frogs in the process as an adult of writing a poem.

Getting to the state of childhood as a purging of the layers of construction imposed by the adult, is romantic and the explicit use of that myth (of the romantic). It is also an investigation through the 'humble' or ordinary experience of the person.

> My sense of the involution of any idea with a story or stories it belongs to, of a universe of contributing contingencies, is such that my sentences knot themselves to bear the import of associations.

'Experience imagined' is the reproducing of/or as an inner world, which was originally and is still recognized as the actual world. This is comparable to Murasaki's fiction. The story takes place, in the sense of creating a place.

> With Dante, I take the literal, the actual, as the primary ground. We ourselves are literal, actual beings. This is the hardest ground for us to know, for we are *of* it—not outside, observing, but inside, experiencing...This creative life is a drive towards the reality of Creation, producing an inner world, an emotional and intellectual fiction, in answer to our awareness of the creative reality of the whole. If the world does not speak to us, we cannot speak with it. If we view the literal as a matter of mere fact, as the positivist does, it is mute. But once we apprehend the literal as a language, once things about us reveal depths and heights of meaning, we are involved in the sense of Creation ourselves, and in our human terms, this is Poetry, Making the inner Fiction of Consciousness. If the actual world be denied as the primary ground and source, that inner fiction can become a fiction of the Unreal, in which not truth but Wish hides.

I would make a comparison and distinction between the notion of "the literal as a matter of mere fact, as the positivist" and a realistically-based modern writing suggested by the example of Murasaki: i.e. suggested by Murasaki's stream of 'realistic' events as void, revealing themselves (in the sense of no explanation or imposition of psychological connections), akin to Benjamin's notion of the communally shared story (i.e. told), which becomes actively integrated as the experience of the listeners.

Experience, by this conception and by definition, is not ideology (i.e. it is not the process of explanation—of being explained—information), or tradition. it is post-Einstein.

The rendition and reception of the experience is linked to a contemplative state in both the storyteller and listener. Benjamin says:

> There is nothing that commends a story to memory more effectively than that chaste compactness which precludes psychological analysis. And the more natural the process by which the storyteller forgoes psychological shading, the greater becomes the story's claim to a place in the memory of the listener, the more completely is it integrated into his own experience, the greater will be his inclination to repeat it to someone else someday, sooner or later. This process of assimilation, which takes place in depth, requires a state of relaxation which is becoming rarer and rarer.

Duncan's work is a variation of such; it is 'experience' as ordinary life of the person as well as in traditions of myth, so that the poems are the analyses of myth itself.

94

Works Cited

Benjamin, Walter. *Illuminations*. New York, N.Y.: Schocken Books, 1969.

Duncan, Robert. *Fictive Certainties*. New York, N.Y.: New Directions, 1985

The Opening of the Field. New York, N.Y.: New Directions, 1960.

Picasso and Anarchism

PICASSO AND ANARCHISM

Re-Ordering the Universe, Picasso and Anarchism, 1897-1914
by Patricia Leighten, 1989, Princeton University Press

This book says that his form is the same as anarchy in that it is a faculty or function.

One familiar with and sympathetic to the plight of the poor and with anarchist analyses of its causes and cure could not innocently choose such subjects for their purely "visual" interest.

These early paintings were not personal.

Anarchist thinker Proudhon says "Society divides itself from art; it puts it outside of real life; it makes of it a means of pleasure and amusement, a pastime, but one which means nothing; it is a superfluity, a luxury, a vanity, a debauchery, an illusion; it is anything you like. It is no longer a faculty or a function, a form of life, an integral part and constituent of existence."

Picasso's collages have a diarist quality, incorporating journals. The content of the newsprint was horrifying descriptions of the war as it was going on. So the collages abandon depth and recognize the conditionality of optical laws.

Such associations embody threats to the civilization represented by the work itself.

He did not replace description with polemic — which is illusion.

Later, with two and three-quarter million civilian and military dead, three-quarters of a million permanently injured, and the entire northeast section of France an utter wasteland, it is not surprising that the prewar assumptions about the civilization that could produce such a destructive cataclysm, the goodness of human nature and earlier anarchist views underwent a crisis of faith. Waldemar George in 1921 pointedly refuted the prewar view of Cubism, adamantly discussing the movement in purely stylistic terms. "Cubism," he wrote, "is an end in itself, a constructive synthesis, an artistic fact, a formal architecture independent of external contingencies, an autonomous language and not a means of representation."

So as not to be a function — either content or form.

waking up dressed having done that
and being tying one's shoe crying in waking
that is extended

not quite that

(they) like reality
as a function

scratch on it

How Phenomena Appear to Unfold

HOW PHENOMENA APPEAR TO UNFOLD

The subject of this talk (in which I will refer to works by Meredith Monk, Philip Whalen, Steve Benson, Norman Fischer, and Alice Notley) is how phenomena appear to unfold in the works mentioned, how one has or creates a sense of history, and therefore creates or seems to create events, or appears to be created by them.

The viewer of anything perceives order later on.

The forms of these works I'm mentioning are modes of awareness and devices of experimentation, the effect or 'function' of which is *not* to be determining order in advance and at the same time to be observing that one is nevertheless doing so.

This is related to the notion that "meaning separates you from reality" (Clark Coolidge).[1]

The impression of history in Monk's *Quarry* is created by simultaneous occurrences, or an appearance of simultaneity, in a number of scenes or locations (viewed by the audience seated above looking down and alongside around a rectangular space, when the work was performed at La Mama theater). Minute daily events start up in these scenes together or consecutively: a group of women eating at a dinner table, an older couple elsewhere in a separate scene exchange shreds of smalltalk, a little girl performed by Meredith Monk lies in the center in bed as if the scenes around her were local viewed by and emanating from her mind; a maid with a broom moves straightening throughout occasionally sitting on a stool fiddling with the radio dials and listening to the radio with the little girl; a boy on a bicycle ringing his bell rides throughout, etc. There is a long early life. The work occurs in three scenes which unfold without a break: Lullaby, March and Requiem. The impression is created that specific individual, in the sense of unrelated, actions are *later* being controlled by dictators in the subsequent unfolding of World War II.

The numerous gestures and scenes of the Lullaby section are held together and at times swept into a motion, as if coming from the little girl in the bed; and from musical repetition such as holding a note, repetition of such dance movements as raising the hands, and triple repetition of phrases or syllables which are sung. There is created an impression of

[1] This essay was originally given as a talk at the Naropa Institute, July 1989, in a session titled "New Forms." This quote comes from a talk given in the same week by Clark Coolidge and Bernadette Mayer.

cause and effect which is not actual. For example, seated in their locations the people in the various separated spots swirl into the same twirling motion, which appears to 'cause' the next action of puffy clouds brought in carried on sticks by others and twirling carried as if swept through. The repetitions in the Lullaby section seem exact, peculiar as if 'life-like,' not 'controlled' in that they are insular (within its moment) as if within the cyclical rhythm of daily life through time; these gestures later appear, in the March section, to have been prior duplications of the later gestures of the dictators. Actions coming from minute specific spots which are not historical causes are later seen to be (in the present) swept in a movement whose apparent source of origination is the dictators. At the same time this impression is seen not to be actual.

For example: in the Lullaby section, the little girl and the maid listen to the radio over which there's a snatch of puppets' voices (children's program) as well as of Hitler-like shouting; in the subsequent dictator scene in the March section, clouds sweep through carried on sticks ushering in a red carpet rolled out on which the dictators strut. The contents of a dictator's conversation are Mickey Mouse, Minny Mouse and Goofy. Things occur before they are announced, thus transpiring from the future to the past. Such as: an attendant tastes food and drops dead from poison. Then "The Dictator's Evening Meal" is announced three time (i.e., after the event and mimicking the form of triple repetitions used in the previous Lullaby section).

Example of a sense of history: the impression of control is created by the overall dictator (performed by Ping Chong) standing or sitting outside or at the head of the rectangular space above, viewing the world (the audience is outside that world, viewing it and part of it). His shouts of echoing cries of war are followed by hand motions slightly duplicating the earlier hand motions of all the people, but now as if directing and drawing the world. He gets to the head of the space by walking down the red carpet of the dictators with nonchalant realistic motions amidst a scene in which everyone else, even those who are themselves dictators, move as if they were puppets. He walks through the subsequent scene of wild mass calisthenics-like military exercises and scenes of the world in war, as an observer with 'realistic' (i.e., appearing to be the source of origination) gestures.

The central scene, the culmination or explosion of energy, is that of Ping Chong's wild echoing shouts of war (followed, after a film, by the scene in which there are calisthenics-military exercises, round-up of the Jews, bodies lying still in death). The film which separates these two violent scenes is silent except for the slight flapping and motion of the frame, i.e., of the motion picture camera which appears to be the source of origination. It is sending out the images from the middle of the work (the central act, titled March, of *Quarry*). A man who earlier ('unidentified') was snapping photographs of the different scenes, has become Ping Chong's aide in the shouting scene, standing silently behind the dictator. We now see who he really is, and (impression of what he really) was. We change our impression of him. The silent film shown after Ping Chong's scene shows figures in white crawling out of a quarry; the camera then sees closer in to bodies in white floating in water, some clinging to logs. Though the lens appears at that moment to be the source of origination sending out images, there are many such 'apparent' sources emanating from the particular scenes in their particular time frames.

As if there are holes all around from which reality is leaking through, and a stream occurring from future to past. The viewer sees the impression of history created, created by oneself though it's occurring outside.

This analysis of *Quarry* is difficult to visualize; but my focus here is literally perspective (how one sees locationally and spatially within the work). Seeing spatially within a *written* work is actively ordering reality. The reader is composing an order in a work. Whalen's 'method' or way of writing is a radical investigation of reality.

I intend the form of the following to be a revelation of his method—by him, as the form of what his work is doing. It is a 'talk' within a talk.

In commenting on Whalen's work, I will use as an example "Birthday Poem." Appearance of phenomena unfolding (how this seems to the viewer, both the speaker in the poem and the reader) is based on the 'physical' location of the viewer. How things appear may be seen from the person actually, that is, 'realistically' being inside locations commenting on the surroundings; or, thoughts or fantasies may occur springing up that will be realms or scenes taking place in themselves; or, ostensibly 'realistic' events may be supposedly (possibly 'actually') seen by the reader or speaker but seen to be 'outside' and really therefore called up thus seemingly created:

And winter just past. What do I see a hundred fish

Survived seventy miles of poisoned water, three million fishermen
Flash silver bug feed flip.

What do I see fish seller grabs a fly out of the air
No place to wipe his fingers

An impression of history is created from the specific, detailed minute scene. Which is not historical cause.

"Birthday Poem" was published in Whalen's selected poems, *Decompressions* (and in *Heavy Breathing*). In the introductory explanatory note to *Decompressions*, Whalen remarks that a poem is going to precede thinking; it is going to think itself, in addition to ripping the poet out of his head:

> think of light wave/particle/bundles being slowly emitted in a pattern from the surface of somebody's face and traveling very slowly through space to mingle with the chemicals of a photographic film and slowly change them so that they in their turn remember the pattern and can reproduce it whenever called upon.

He quotes a passage from Stein's essay "Narration" citing the passage as a more exact expression of this conception:

> If you exist any day you are not the same as any other day no nor any minute of the day because you have inside you being existing. Anybody who is existing and anybody really anybody is existing anybody really is that.
> But anything happening well the inside and the outside are not the inside and the outside inside.
> Let me do that again. The inside and the outside, the outside which is outside and the inside which is inside are not when they are inside and outside are not inside in short they are not existing, that is inside, and when the outside is entirely outside that is it is not at all inside then it is not at all inside and so it is not existing. Do you not see what a newspaper is and perhaps history.

Whalen's view that the poem precedes thinking is comparable to Meredith Monk's form: the specific locations which are entirely inside appear to give rise to the outside. This process is later seen to be the same as the outside.

"I did not have the idea Now today I'm going to manufacture this poem."

I asked Whalen a few questions about his writing process, recording our conversation on tape. (I will quote some of his responses. I have arranged them taking them out of the order in which I asked the questions.) He described his mode of composition as writing long-hand in a notebook, sometimes accompanying the writing with drawings. About structure:

> The structure is made up to fit whatever suits me on the page. How it looks. Because you know for all practical purposes I never typed anything on the page; I always wrote everything long-hand and typed it later. It looks one way when it's written and another way when it's typed. If I don't like the way the linebreaks go I might change and other times not change it for anything. Certainly like Olson says, the typewriter has an influence on anything you write, but I got around that by always writing in long-hand. So I could write all over the page or around the edges of it.

He would look at the accumulated material in a notebook sometimes months after fragments were written, type the bits on separate pieces of paper, and put these on the floor to see what was there and what went together: "Sometimes on different days, on different months in a notebook. And then I'd look at these things and be typing it up out of a notebook and saw patterns in it all through and decided this part here was going to follow something else or not. And I can't explain. It was a poetical phrenzy."

Asked whether the accumulated material would sometimes go into different works, he answered affirmatively: "Some things arrive and they're done. You might make minor alterations. But they're done. Eight or fourteen lines. And that's the end of it. You can see that. And so that kind you can leave alone. Other times you have stuff that looks like it's not all there, and so you have to leave it and read it later."

It might be the circumstance of Donald Allen asking for a book. Whalen would look through his notebooks. He might find single objects and type those up:

> And then you could see that there were fragments of something. And those fragments go down on the floor. And you find out that something you wrote last year and something you wrote five minutes ago are part of the same news. But it is always surprising to see that you have been doing this; that you have been through, over a space of time, been thinking about the same

thing, or writing in circles around something. And if you tie it all together, it makes up a thing.

If there appeared to be a spot that looked vacant in the poem after it was typed, he might write something right then to put in there. Other times, he would cut material. He went out on walks carrying a notebook. He tended to spend two or three hours in the morning in which he didn't do anything except sit with a blank piece of paper. The poem, for example, titled "Dream" (in *On Bear's Head*) was a rendition as exact as possible of an actual dream, as just that.

> It was something I just *did*. It was exciting to keep on going to see what could happen, what I could come up with. Sometimes I would write something and I would just turn the page and forget it. And without thinking about it and write more stuff and maybe days later I might be thumbing through the stuff and wonder where did *that* come from? So, I don't know any more about it than that, except like I said in the seminar about Ted (Berrigan) I had the same experience of reading intensively and pretty soon your head gets all packed with material of all kinds and some of it leaks out into what *you're* working on in that the trivia comes out between *your* lines, or in quotes or whatever. And at that time, up until a few years ago anyway, I used to read you know quite extensively and for long periods of time and be always carrying a book around with me, of some kind or another. And in the last— say from 1986 or so—it's been more and more difficult to read. So I can't do that any more. It makes me very nervous that I can't read and it's very hard to write because if I'm not careful the lines start either crossing each other or dangling on the page. So I might be having to go into typing everything; and that prospect is not at all pleasant because I like the feeling of writing with the pen.

The mode of the work is not collage. It is an observation of fragments as they come up in a time period. "These long poems had to be put together literally on the floor, pasting and gluing."

"Birthday Poem" took two years to be completed; it was begun in Kyoto in 1967, continued in San Francisco and finished in Kyoto in 1969: "It would be in several notebooks. To get all of the material that I figured was going to be this thing after it was done. After I had it all there, and I looked at it all and I said Oh this is what there is there, that's a whole thing there, and it all connects together doesn't it." Asked about planning, whether there was a sense in advance of the completion or the shape of the poem: "I didn't know, not until I had it on the floor." "Birthday Poem" was typed and considered or 'composed' at the end of two years; it existed, as it went along, only as its unexamined accumulation in the notebook.

The fragments of his poems are maintained as they were variously written in their time periods.

The writing as simply a mode of seeing what comes up in a time period is similar to the sense in *Quarry* of reality leaking through from all around in a present, and created from future to past. The poem thinks itself, being ahead of the person.

What occurs is in the middle of the work (within the line). "It has a thing inside the line the way the words go together. Rhythmical thing in the back of my mind somewhere and I'm very finicky about how the end of one word and beginning of another are going together."

Asked whether he used a formal pattern of fugues, or his own pattern:

> My own pattern. Not necessarily having to do with fugues, but it's inter-weaving of different strands of ideas or notes, sounds that come around and about and all make a strange harmony. Somehow the overall object has its own proportions and its own working parts inside but it's hard to see 'em I think. Some people do and they like it and others say Now why did you do that? And if they say that you're out of luck. It's like you can't explain a joke. You can't explain jazz. And you do it because it's fun, for the excitement of doing it.

Asked about the relation of the inside and the outside as articulated in the quote from Stein, Whalen commented on the passage:

> how the inside is really inside and the outside is really outside. It's all about psychology and it has some connection also with the way Buddhist psychol-ogy looks at things; how you eventually find out the outside is really inside. How you're making the world you're making things; that your sense is hooked up to your perception, sense of hearing is connected to your ears and your ears are connected to sounds and it's all totally mixed up. You can't say there's something out there. It's all inside. I don't know that I really got into that so much in any of my work.

(The following is my interpretation). The speaker, the person writing the poem appears to be duplicating things, but these things are actually inside *him*. This is also true of others.

There is a long present-time early life. Which really means that the action, or apparent source of origination—in the poem, and possibly in the sense of actual memory or life—is in the future.

> Leads (*via* Hollywood) into strange Kyoto present memory
> Flying every day for many months early morning B-17
>   (TOMORROW?)
> My name was Dumbo then, leather skin high-altitude elephant,
>   dangling oxygen trunk
>   (TOMORROW EARLY)
> pink hydraulic hairoil fluid
> Ethyl-ester perfume airplane fuel for cigaret lighter
> Oxygen for hangover
>   (A HOME IN THE ARMY)
> Fall asleep reading Whitman Civil War riding in the greenhouse
>   high above the Chocolate Mountains
> All one short enormous life
>   how possible went?
> Shall I be late tomorrow?
>   (EARLY. SEVEN DAYS A WEEK.)
>   with Jeanette MacDonald's husband
>   (SMILIN' THROUGH)
>   for an airplane driver
> How did I ever get here? Enormous possibilities all miscarried
> Long impossible early life
>   bestowed becalmed bedizened
> Lovely desert mornings early every day
> Mornings early every flying day twenty-three years ago

That the action is early (is in the beginning) means the appearance of cause and effect, which is not actual.

> Always volunteer; never perform. This is benevolence. This is correction of the Will. Ted Williams went and spit on the grass.
> Go now and write properly.

The unfolding of the phenomena of the poem occurs as a stream of images, scenes, comments, and personages from history, radio, and the movies. The depiction (beginning on the tenth page of the poem, p. 62 of *Decompressions*) of the corruption and manipulation, killing and bamboozling on the part of governments, politicians and banks is preceded by the image of a thin membrane being pushed from inside beyond the breaking point. In the 'tyrant passages,' the creation of history, as the attachment to and reflexion of others' opinions, is seen to be not actual. Addressing friends, Governments, and Policemen:

> Take a hoop and roll it
>
> I laugh at you; I die and live continually
> Imagining I care for you, you care for me
>
> Lies & fraud
> Nothing's genuine except imagination who creates
> Whether we will or no: for fun
> For boredom. For nothing.
> I chose to appear in this place, to come to your party
> I do it on purpose, over and over again
> I hate parties, I always have a good time
> And it always takes hours for me to recover my sanity
> I go there to reassure you that the world is impractical
> Magic and lunacy, poetry spells and music
>
> I don't even realize you don't understand that you don't need
> The help that I imagine you need I imagine I bring
>
> Imagining I (but that is only you:
> All of us projections overlapping real transparent scene)
> I must act right, I must intend right even when there's
> No such thing as I or right I must choose correctly
> Keep these muscles practising, always hit the right key
> I can read the score perfectly well,
> Nerves and coordination perfectly fine
> Only a temporary case of mistaken identity
> Claude Raines. Bette Davis. Herbert Marshall. Monty Woolley.
> George Sanders. Edith Sitwell. Lionel Barrymore. Ethel Barrymore.

The passages which are the rendition of and diatribe on the power of government and tyrants are a culmination of resonance in the poem, in that an engagement with this is the direction in which the poem appears to have been moving (when one is reading those passages).

Whalen does not 'define' the writing. "Do you conceive of writing as being a meditation?"

> No. No, no, no. It's a form of amusement, a form of excitement, a form of—it's just something that's fun to do; you just do it, or not. And it makes me very nervous not to be doing it.

111

> You know a lot of the time I used to sit and make pictures in a notebook. I can dig up the notebooks that that stuff came out of and show you. Sometimes there'd be you know a few lines of something that eventually gets into print. And it's a mixture of things. And so if I just say it's raining today, I'm not going to copy that out on the typewriter. Unless I really feel that I have to somehow. It's very difficult to talk about because I don't *know* what I'm doing until after it's done' and then after it's done it's interesting or not. And that's all.

The mode of constructing by laying the pages on the floor is an 'objective' experiment. This is without any proposition that the writer is able to remove himself from the writing as a kind of objective camera-lens-like analysis of reality (a concept in writing which would actually be the opposite, constituting a hidden narrator).

Compare to the current view of 'radical questioning of subjectivity' as analysis in the writing which is (supposedly) thereby free of social construction; that is analysis (of subjectivity) which implies a critique of the conception of the unified subject. Yet as a concept of 'objectivity,' the view (the analysis) itself *constitutes* a unified subject.

Anyone's perception of cause and effect, and their ordering in the writing, is a conception of the unfolding of phenomena. It is oneself, and is the recreation and examination of that. There is no authority, no objectivity.

The mind is vacant containing trivia, memories, dreams, opinions. Asked whether part of the purpose in a poem is to get it, the 'trivia' and associations, out there to see what one is doing with it, Whalen replied:

> Well, the thing is I'm not doing anything with it until it's on paper. And some of the stuff that gets on the paper I don't find interesting. Or it has no bounce to it or no rhythm to it. But certain things come up, like the line Louis remembered about "With your finger on the throttle and your foot upon the treadle of the clutch" how all those l and t and d sounds run together in such a funny way. It just happened; although that became a part of a much longer piece, but it was once a stray, almost a poem itself.

(My interpretation:). There is only something when it's written, when it's on paper. According to Whalen in the introduction, "By strict attention to (and application of) a version of logic and empiricism and the experimental method," we have created a luxurious life for a few who control the money machine. Whalen's process is a form of reverse empiricism. In his writing, the 'causes of history' (of or in the poem) do not actually lie in the specific detailed scenes, thoughts, or words. Words, put out there, are vacant (in the sense of the mind getting rid of the words, as in the lines of the poem "The Best of It:" "Get the words out of my head / Lewis looked at me one day and yelled, / 'Look at your head. You got all those words in there! / Your head is full of words!' "). Scenes and words occur past the various 'culminations.' The following is one scene, viewed after the rendition of or diatribe on governments and tyrants. It is not the outcome of either that phenomena or of the diatribe. It (and the speaker) appear(s) to be 'free.'

> A green hole in the distance
> Green diamond, beryl, emerald.
> Professors and students now appear in
> Brilliant feathers, plumes, gems, enamels
> (Black palm fronds)
> Each one is different. What is it they are eating.
> Word word word word word click.

Putting the words outside is related to the writing being ahead of or preceding the person.

The writing is a mode, not a system. 'Apparent' source(s) of origination in the writing are the individual locations or 'selves' and scenes, the future creating the past.[2] All these loci are "projections overlapping real transparent scene" like a motion picture camera which sends out images and also sees them. That 'real' transparent scene is constant movement *within* time: "Double-motion projection of streetcar (moving water moving along / steel tracks the moving bridge."

In the original performance of Steve Benson's work "Back" (included in *Reverse Order*), a xeroxed text was passed out to the audience. Benson 'read' it duplicating phrases from it and gradually beginning to diverge by commenting, extrapolating and interweaving with it to include the moment in which the event was occurring. The event was taped. The later

---

[2] When after writing this talk I described this sense in his writing and in Monk's work, Whalen appeared startled. He said, (Zen Master) "Dōgen said the future creates the past." Him not having been completely aware of this at the time of writing the poem—is an example of the future creating the past.

written text is a compilation including that event, which comments on itself as performance; the developing work is 'read' and changed in the process, so that it is literally *on* itself as in the moment of the speaker's and audience's concentration—on one separating from oneself and so from concentration to be right there next to 'experience.' The attention of the mind (of either the speaker's, or the reader's or listener's) in reading the text or during the performance, is neither in nor outside that experience. As described in a line from Benson's poem "Reverse Order," this is concentration "that slumbers at the edges of intention, too supple finally for either on or off." "Back" is a stream of associations and "translators" (which are the speaker, the different time frames and their context of events).

The writing is extended in sometimes very ordinary subject matter and surface in which divergence from the self (viewer or speaker) and concentration on that becomes apparent.

Benson's *Blue Book* is a collection of experimental works which are forms of improvisational dialogue—of the inside speaking to the inside to eventually perceive the inside and outside as the same.

The works in *Blue Book* are a series of devices; the title piece, "Blue Books," was composed by filling up fifty examination books, with the intention of writing in a don't-look back mode to see what would occur and without presuming any option of revision. Benson describes the open-ended, improvisational nature of the project as not insuring any particular quality of spontaneity or passion, self-consciousness or lack of that: "I only assumed that I didn't know what I would write, one moment (word, line, phrase, sentence) to the next, or one day (sitting, book) to the next." In regard to the risk of self-indulgence or failure, "I accepted this in a spirit of stubborn resistance to ideals of quality. I was impatient and dissatisfied with just about any criteria for valuing the work as 'finished,' and glad to feel that I could and would screw it up." The piece "Blue Books" is actually selections excerpted from the complete project.

He writes in that particular piece without stopping, to see what occurs. It is as if looking into a mirror and writing from that. The writing is the overlap—ostensibly the point of agreement or "point of no appearance":

    you think—no perspective,
    they say. We keep moving—trying
    to head down that dividing line,
    disappearing point—what's it

called? Point of no appearance,
yet it seems the crux of reality
seen with a one...Vanishing—
When you only have a one-vanishing-
point perspective, you need to
vanish straight, so you don't
radiate, and distribute annihilation
all over the place

The lens examining the lens, the mind examining the mind is the point of no appearance. The writing device is viewed as the lens:

staying behind the function of its
lens, the will is positioned, revealing
its framing, holding ground, but no
moving, except that pushing out
through, the method so stationary
the instrument moving, arbitrarily
veering around, pushing, the earth
has no center any more against the
eyes' mind, the function of the
relation between the camera and
photographer's eye..

Distinctions of quality as to 'good' poetic form are broken down in favor of this articulated function of observation of phenomena. Benson's de-emphasis of an intention of 'art' in his notes to *Blue Book* implies a critique of his own method; the effect of writing is not essence, but rather the streams of things aligning in and out of consciousness. A conception of essence is actually a fiction of dialogue:

but whether what I do is any better done
than anything or anybody else's doing of it
if there is or were an identity to be made
between projects, as, essence we're all doing
the same or one actual thing, I doubt it,
except surviving...

Form in writing does not define. One does not define 'innovation' in advance. 'Innovation' is not a particular syntax.

Benson's introductory notes describe how he composed each of the projects in the book. The descriptions are part of the works, as a means of

115

enabling the reader to duplicate the act or 'performance' of them. They are also separate, 'outside' the works. They precede and/or follow the works.

"The Town of He," for example, was composed by memorizing two pages each from five texts (including Thoreau's "Civil Disobedience," Huizinga's essay on Abelard, and Johnson's *Life of Swift*). The author spent two months memorizing and practicing recombining the material, and in performance spoke out from memory words, phrases and sentences of the texts as they occurred to him:

> As in effect I was reading off my memory, the appearance was of a recitation; since I was choosing and often pausing in deliberation or patient vacancy, the sensation of an unforseeable and unrepeatable presentation was palpable as well.

"The Town of He" is indicative of the conceptual nature of this body of work. This particular text as written may not be as interesting as the conception of it. His work is not its sound pattern, for example. The poem's interest is in the idea of an act which cannot be repeated. It is another form of the dialogue (in which the listener(s) is self and audience) as an act.

Blue Book is not examples of automatic writing. What's occurring is in its intention, its 'vision.'

Norman Fischer's *Turn Left In Order To Go Right* has passages of prose in which there is movement that throughout the extended work or book is contrapuntal to the interspersed, fairly short-lined poems. There appears to be a sweep of movement through the 'book,' as well as within the individual works. The reader or the speaker in it has the illusion of being within the individual increments (which do not appear to contain or to be change, as they tend to be mere observations or statements about people and events; as such they are the *abstractions* of events); at some point, without knowing when this has occurred, the viewer perceives being already outside of a stream of such increments, as if change has already taken place. The following is a description of this process, description of movement as such being the mode of the increments of the writing. The writing is not 'descriptive;' nothing is described. This passage is from "Poem for Bach's Three Hundredth Birthday," which Fischer describes in a note as having been composed in contrapuntal form:

> The kids' lives do go on in a marvelous way despite all. There's a blind

energy there you have to marvel at, how they know exactly what they want (although of course they have no idea how to get it) from the very beginning, and how their little bodies stretch forward toward tomorrow, sensing, or maybe literally even smelling, destiny standing there in an overcoat reading a newspaper at the corner where the express bus stops. They are born with such a dramatic sense of definitiveness. They don't necessarily want to be here but something propels them forward in tremendous struggle they come inch by inch coursed along by some grand movement like the sea in a very clear direction out into the harshness. ...until bit by bit this elemental quality leaves them, or rather doesn't really leave them so much as get defined out; still there but unnoticed. And the word 'elemental' isn't it either, but rather points us in exactly the wrong direction. All the words, in fact, are the wrong ones: magical, and all we've got, but essentially wrong, because they point to something, when really there isn't anything.

The description of the movement is all that appears to be there. Akin to Benson's application of his writing as a lens, Fischer is using the very element of description, the warp of abstraction as the writing's means of sight. The matter of the work is ordinary, crucial experience (such as the death of one's parent). From the poem "For Your Own Good:"

But if I try to find myself it is impossible, because like a fingertip that cannot touch itself or a knife that cannot cut itself I cannot see myself I can only see an abstraction, glass, outside of which I am placed in thought, in language. I only imagine myself to continue. In actuality I must stop and recreate myself over again. Time doesn't go by I go by. I don't see anything, anything sees me. Before I arrive I'm already there. Before I leave I've already returned. The sentence writes itself, refracts itself and unwinds. So sentence is thus and for the sentence sight.

The capacity of the sentence to be "sight" is derived from it being vacant, from it not being skilled as artful 'composition' (as in the comment, "The trouble with us is we know exactly what we are doing. We are skilled and we cannot turn back."). This refers to the construction (i.e. prior description) of a society, world, a sense of an individual's life. The effect of an unrefined or apparently unedited, crude text which is doing a description of its process or movement is not being that.

Everything human beings stand for assumes conclusions and improvements, and we keep going over and over the text, replacing old parts with new, adjusting an idling screw, breaking off an old nut, sharpening up the teeth of the gears. That way we produce an activity whose hum resonates precisely with a tone we've had in our head since the beginning, and we feel a positive sense of well being that is almost transcendant.

It doesn't matter if the sentence has 'sight:' The poem is not a product—it is not any *thing*. This is writing which is a form of speaking to oneself, to the one who's speaking—until it is neither: "Right through the spaces between the buttons on the shirt. Trees swish. Birds don't want to fly. Why is not an element of time. Time matters, is matter. Is organized like a lark, on a lark."

The form of Alice Notley's poem "White Phosphorus" is phrases and words in quotation marks, beside each other in stanzas; they are in quotes because it is what we say, it is a mask, it is outside, and yet it is also "center of senses," "center of, moment."

The 'context' is that of a brother actually having died from having been in the war in Vietnam. His death has occurred in the present long after that war. The context is the war. It is the moment "before we were born?"; after death; inside *this* moment; it is "seen through his eyes"; actual death; it is what people say, which is history.

"In this moment" "before" "anyone, ever" "died" "before we were born?"
"in this moment forever before" "before we went to a war"
"Before we died" "In this moment, now" "In this moment before, it is
not before" "In this very moment" "where is it" "where we
haven't died" "or died inside" "In this moment we haven't" "in this
moment, no one" "in this moment, no one has ever, died" ("But I have
been born") "in this moment" "where, where is it" "in moment" "who's
    here"
"Catch it catch it" "moment where we are" "merely as it is autonomous,"

The phrases are in the frames of their quotes. The moments or particles are autonomous, existing separately beside each other in the poem which is without a frame (without quotes).

(knowledge, so endless'' "is nothing") "A war" "more news, more
to know about, to know" "Excuse for anger" "indignation" "you can still
keep your money" "know the terms of news" "terms" "Know what news
    knows"

"What words know" "Do words know?" "No they don't, only flesh knows
    only
soul knows" "in the words" "A mask is rigid" "on warm flesh on
dreaming mind" "on fleshly mind" "rigid" "But my brother now is
nature, pure nature" "however that be" "Or I have dreamed so" "Owl,
not an albatross" "He's an owl," "not an albatross" "I have twice
"dreamed that Al" "is an owl" "intricate with" "feathers" "texture of

The idea of history—which has been created by the "country," by
"America," "soldiers," "us"—has become a form 'within' the context of
the poem (it is its inside). It is our view of it. The 'form' has become an
apparatus, a device for transforming actual life and death.

I am concerned in my own work with the sense that phenomena appear
to unfold. (What is it or) how is it that the viewer sees the impression of
history created, created by oneself though it's occurring outside?

Multiple perspective (in these works), in which the viewer and
speaker are 'within' (being its inside) the work, allows reality to leak from
many holes all around. As (spatially) infinity is all around one, it creates
a perspective that is socially democratic, individual (in the sense of
specific) and limitless.

Leslie Scalapino was born in Santa Barbara, California, and raised in Berkeley. She was educated at Berkeley High School and Reed College; and received an M.A. from the UC Berkeley English Department (an experience so awful that it has not yet been erased from memory). She has seven books of poetry including *Considering how exaggerated music is* (1982), *that they were at the beach—aeolotropic series* (1985), and *way* (1988); these were published by North Point Press. *way* received the American Book Award from the Before Columbus Foundation, the Lawrence Lipton Prize, and the San Francisco State Poetry Center Award. Scalapino received NEA grants for poetry in 1976 and 1986. She has had many part-time jobs and traveled in Asia, Africa, and Europe; most recently in India and Japan (1986) and Egypt, Yemen, Sudan, and Italy (1988). She lives happily with Tom White. Her poetic plays have been performed by the Poets Theater in San Francisco and Los Angeles and the Eye and Ear Theater in New York.

POTES AND POETS PRESS PUBLICATIONS

Miekal And, *Book 7, Samsara Congeries*
Bruce Andrews, *Excommunicate*
Bruce Andrews, from *Shut Up*
Todd Baron, *dark as a hat*
Dennis Barone, *Forms / Froms*
Dennis Barone, *The World / The Possibility*
Lee Bartlett, *Red Scare*
Beau Beausoleil, *in case / this way two things fell*
Steve Benson, *Reverse Order*
Steve Benson, *Two Works Based on Performance*
Brita Bergland, *form is bidden*
Charles Bernstein, *Amblyopia*
Charles Bernstein, *Conversation with Henry Hills*
Charles Bernstein, *disfrutes*
Julia Blumenreich, *Parallelism*
John Byrum, *Cells*
Abigail Child, *A Motive for Mayhem*
Norma Cole, *Metamorphopsia*
Clark Coolidge, *A Geology*
Clark Coolidge, *The Symphony*
Cid Corman, *Essay on Poetry*
Cid Corman, *Root Song*
Beverly Dahlen, *A Reading (11-17)*
Tina Darragh, *a(gain)²st the odds*
Tina Darragh, *Exposed Faces*
Alan Davies, *a an av es*
Alan Davies, *Mnemonotechnics*
Alan Davies, *Riot Now*
Jean Day, from *No Springs Trail*
Ray DiPalma, *The Jukebox of Memnon*
Ray DiPalma, *New Poems*
Rachel Blau DuPlessis, *Drafts #8 and #9*
Rachel Blau DuPlessis, *Tabula Rosa*
Johanna Drucker, from *Bookscape*
Theodore Enslin, *Case Book*
Theodore Enslin, *Meditations on Varied Grounds*
Theodore Enslin, *September's Bonfire*
Norman Fischer, *The Devices*
Steven Forth, *Calls This*
Peter Ganick, *Met Honest Stanzas*
Peter Ganick, *Rectangular Morning Poem*
Peter Ganick, *Two Space Six*
Robert Grenier, *What I Believe*
Carla Harryman, *Vice*

Carla Harryman, *The Words*
Susan Howe, *Federalist 10*
Janet Hunter, *in the absence of alphabets*
P. Inman, *backbite*
P. Inman, *Think of One*
P. Inman, *waver*
Andrew Levy, *Reading Places, Reading Times*
Jackson MacLow, *Prose & Verse from the Early 80's*
Barbara Moraff, *Learning to Move*
Janette Orr, *The Balcony of Escape*
Gil Ott, *Public Domain*
Maureen Owen, *Imaginary Income*
Keith Rahmings, *Printouts*
Dan Raphael, *The Matter What Is*
Dan Raphael, *Oops Gotta Go*
Dan Raphael, *Zone du Jour*
Stephen Ratcliffe, *Sonnets*
Joan Retallack, *Western Civ Cont'd*
Maria Richard, *Secondary Image / Whisper Omega*
Susan Roberts, *cherries in the afternoon*
Kit Robinson, *Up Early*
Leslie Scalapino, *clarinet part I heard*
Laurie Schneider, *Pieces of Two*
Gail Sher, *w/*
James Sherry, *Lazy Sonnets*
Ron Silliman, *B A R T*
Ron Silliman, *Lit*
Ron Silliman, from *Paradise*
Pete Spence, *Almanak*
Pete Spence, *Elaborate at the Outline*
Diane Ward, *Being Another / Locating in the World*
Craig Watson, *The Asks*
Hannah Weiner, *Nijole's House*

Potes & Poets Press, Inc.
181 Edgemont Avenue
Elmwood CT 06110